CW01307940

WHEELSONG POETRY ANTHOLOGY 6

Edited by

Steve Wheeler
Matt Elmore
Nadia Martelli

First published by
Wheelsong Books
4 Willow Close,
Plymouth PL3 6EY,
United Kingdom

© Wheelsong Poetry, 2025

The right of all featured poets to be identified as the authors of this work have been asserted by them in accordance with the Copyright, Designs and Patents Act of 1988.

Book design and cover Art © Steve Wheeler, 2025
Cover Photography © Kelly Cheek Rodriguez
First published in 2025

All rights reserved. Except as permitted under current legislation no part of this work may be photocopied, stored in a retrieval system, published, performed in public, adapted, broadcast, transmitted, recorded or reproduced in any form or by any means, without the prior permission of the copyright owners. Any enquiries should be addressed
to Wheelsong Books.

Softcover Print ISBN: 979-8-28210-067-9

*"Poetry is just the evidence of life.
If your life is burning well,
poetry is just the ash."*

—Leonard Cohen

FUNDRAISING IN AID OF

Save the Children

Contents

Foreword	Steve Wheeler	17
Hello	Kevin Francis	19
The Sky	Mieczyslaw Kasprzyk	20
Time	Brygida Błażewicz	20
Weeping Willow	Catherine A. MacKenzie	21
Deeper than any Blade	Emile Pinet	21
In Plain Sight	Archie Papa	22
My Clay, My Makers	Larry Bailie	22
We have the Poets	Steve Wheeler	23
Sunburst	Sarah Sansbury	23
Burning Memories	Karen Bessette	24
The Soul of a Poet	W. Fields	24
In 50 Years	Natasha Browne	25
Night Waits	Linda Adelia Powers	27
The Burning Truth	Ashly Tenini	27
Stolen Words	Sarah Jane Holden	28
God's Garden	Gregory Richard Barden	28
Empty Spaces	David Cragg	29
Burned in a Dream	Nadia Martelli	29
Fragility of Being	Michael Hukkanen	30
Freeze Frame	Tracy Taylor	30
The Bridge I Trace	Jodeci Flores	31
Wonder in Our Hearts	Larry Bailie	32
The Beach	D. A. Simpson	33
Leeward	Shirley Rose	34
The Sleeper in the Vale	Robert Atkins	35
Inviting Waters	Charlene Phare	35
Summer Sojourns	Tanya Raval	36
Patchwork	Kendra Bower	36
The Golden Ribbons of the World	Victoria Puckering	37
Decline and Fall	Terry Bridges	37
A Raven	Brygida Błażewicz	38
Inner Storm	Rose Marie Streeter	38
Practical Physics	Steve Wheeler	39

Bluster will Blister	Kwaku Adjei-Fobi	39
Accumulation	Tom Cleary	40
It never did Me no Harm	Richard de Bulat	40
Are You…	Tom Watkins	41
My Neurodivergent Brain	Iain Strachan	43
Feeling of Exile	Famara S. Sock	44
Somewhere in-between	Hayley Sejberg	44
Grains of Dust	D. A. Simpson	45
Daddy's Little Girl	Larry Bracey	46
We are not the Broken Things…	Zac Warden	47
Wren	James Alexander Crown	48
Hungry Lullaby	Ryan Morgan	49
Alchemystical	Scot A. Buffington	50
Poetically Country	Rose Marie Streeter	51
Ode to Us	Anna Treasure	52
Once More	Archie Papa	54
A Photo of You	Richard de Bulat	54
Gift	R. David Fletcher	55
My Soul	J. P. Hayter	55
Tonight	Karen Bessette	56
Unseen	Roger Simpson	56
Ubiquitous	Lorna McLaren	57
A Single Word	Michael Hukkanen	57
a look before my leap	Matt Elmore	58
Hope's Shadow	Martha M. Miller	58
Through their Gaze	Ashly Tenini	59
A Lovers' Tiff	Stephen James Smith	60
Echoes	Kendra Bower	61
My Love for Freedom	Rafik Romdhani	62
She Dreams	Michelle Tarbin	63
Endless Breath	Karin J. Hobson	64
Jealousy Station	Peter Rivers	65
Man	W. Fields	66
Chosen	Alan Sharkey	67
Love	Melissa Stegall	67
No Words	Tracy Taylor	68
In the Palm of My Hand	Fouzia Sheikh	69
Ore	Corey Reynolds	70
Until the River Ends	Dale Parsons	70

I'll Water Your Flowers	Mike Rose	71
To Face My Fading Light	Peter Rivers	72
Pearls	Ian Cave	73
Moonings	Scot A. Buffington	74
My Pen Friend	Thomas B. Maxwell	75
Spring Sun and Sadness	Susanne West	76
Wish I had a Home like You	Christine Gallant	76
Mystical	R. David Fletcher	77
Women	Tanya Raval	77
I Dreamed of Blue	Jennifer M. Nichols	78
The Perfect Companion	Nadia Martelli	78
Falling Home	Tracey Buster & Tim Queen	79
Colors of Love	Patricia Woosley	80
Seaside Senses	Micheal Jean Laswell	80
Late Night on the River	Mike Rose	81
Mum	Beth Anne Nigro	82
Grand Stage	Roland Wayne Bebler	83
Cosmic Conformity	Stephen James Smith	84
Caliginous Saunter	Karin J. Hobson	85
Soliloquizing	Kwaku Adjei-Fobi	85
Romanesque	Chuck Porretto	86
When it Started	Larry Bailie	87
That's Just Dad	Tracy Taylor	88
My Heart	Catherine A. MacKenzie	88
Maundy	Robert Atkins	89
Too Much Grey	Valerie Dohren	90
Schumann Frequency	Ryan Morgan	91
Find Home	Patrick Darnell	91
Coming Light	Trude Foster	92
Snowfall	Micheal Jean Laswell	92
What Would You Do?	Carol Lease	93
Icarus	Stephen W. Atkinson	93
Fix You	J. Henry DeKnight	94
Caryatids	Linda Adelia Powers	95
Heartbreak	James Alexander Crown	96
Time is Rhyme	Catherine A. MacKenzie	97
Let's Dance to Peace	Tracy Murphy	97
If Poetry was a Crime	Jessica F. C. Magalhães	98
Water, Hills, War	Patrick Darnell	99
Sands of Time	Gemma Tansey	100

Feels	Simon Drake	101
Span of Life	Gregory Richard Barden	102
The Meadow	George Valler	102
Opposites	Mike Rose	103
Kaleidoscope Visions	Lorna McLaren	104
If Putin liked Children's Books	Hayley Sejberg	104
Live Every Day	Richard Harries	105
Yellow Bands	John C. Algar	106
Speculation	Rachel Yarworth	106
Kensington Avenue	Charles P. Howes	107
Society	Bruce S. Hart	108
Unseen	Stephen W. Atkinson	108
Unsatisfied Desires	Anita Chechi	109
Waxing Moon	Tom Cleary	109
Listen to a Stream	Chuck Porretto	110
I Will Find You	Sheila Grenon	111
Journey	Moazzem Hossain	112
A Shadowy Room	Kevin Francis	113
Concrete Jungle	Donna Smith	113
Motherhood: Unfiltered	Jodeci Flores	114
What is it Like?	Garrie Grant	115
Getting to the Other Side	Rachel Yarworth	116
A Dream in a Bookcase	Rafik Romdhani	117
Sandstone Ghosts	Angela Brown	117
The Dawn River	Moazzem Hossain	119
Pink Moon	Tracey Buster & Tim Queen	120
Alcatraz	Simon Drake	121
Love Beats	Sharon Toner	122
Live Alone	Rafik Romdhani	123
Gloom Quickens	Martha M. Miller	123
Dancing into the Uncertainty	Iain Strachan	124
Carcassonne	Kate Cameron	125
Village of the Lost	Lorna McLaren	126
Connecting Dots	Natasha Browne	127
A Mile in Your Shoes	Larry Bracey	128
Chainsaws	Neil Mason	128
Another Soul's Shoes	Graeme Stokes	129
The Abolition of Warmth	Brandon Adam Haven	130
Beat and Breath	David Catterton Grantz	131

Title	Author	Page
The Roots of the Soul	Anemone Rosendal	132
Haunted Verses	Jou Wilder	132
The Bewitching Hour	Jamie Willis	133
The Flower	Mark Heathcote	134
The Sea of Dreams	Colin Hunt	135
Dawn of Hope	Scott Barnett	136
Contrast	Richard Harries	137
Chaotic World	Ceba Sanelisiwe	137
Defying the Odds	Donna Smith	138
A Poem Without Words	Jessica F. C. Magalhães	139
Midwinter Lives	Sean Timms	139
The Art of Conditioning	Taylore Juliet Ashton	140
Mature Outrage	Martha M. Miller	141
Meetings	Shweta Bhide	142
Metamorphic	Dale Parsons	142
triolet o' chocolates	Matt Elmore	143
Taraxacum	Jamie Willis	143
The Pain of the Oyster's Pearl	Sharon Toner	144
Fiesta of Sunset	Sean Timms	144
Nothing	Linda Falter	145
Angel of Death	Brandon Adam Haven	145
My Son of Sunshine	Eric Aguilar	146
When the Storm was Over	Kate Cameron	147
The Church	George Valler	147
Poetry is Me	Graeme Stokes	148
The River	J. P. Hayter	149
Are You Hiding Like Me?	Angela Brown	150
September	Roland Wayne Bebler	151
Where You End and I Begin	Matthew Burgio	151
Burning Absence	Stephen James Smith	152
Purplicity	Sarah Sansbury	153
Eclipse	Bruce S. Hart	153
Confession	Kendra Bower	154
The Moment is Gone	Steve Wheeler	155
22-Minute Power Cut	Ryan Morgan	156
Lion	James Alexander Crown	157
The Gap	Lorna Caizley	158
Evil	Robert Atkins	158
View from a Vase	Tom Cleary	159

Dangling Ringlets in Spring's Hair	Sean Timms	159
Smells	Gemma Tansey	160
Weightless Anchor	Jou Wilder	161
Digital Dementia	Iain Strachan	162
Love Rocks	Linda Falter	163
A Poet Writes	Fouzia Sheikh	164
Glide	Tracey Buster & Tim Queen	165
Acta Non Verba	Charlene Phare	166
Fall of a Good Man	John M. Wright	167
Swan Song	Zac Warden	168
A Triumph of Bees on Alkanet	Kate Cameron	169
The Thought of You	Valerie Dohren	170
Isles of Love	Brandon Adam Haven	171
January Day	Joan Audette	171
The Cross	Ian Cave	172
Necromancing	Jamie Willis	173
A Walk Through Silence	Tom Watkins	174
Endless Possibilities	Emile Pinet	175
Layers	Zac Warden	176
What Happiness is	Ashly Tenini	178
Poet's Teatime	Neil Mason	179
Blurred Image	Joan Audette	179
The Merry Maidens	Ian Cave	180
Where have I held your Hand?	Kevin Francis	180
Name that Movie	Patrick Darnell	181
Through the Tears	Eric Aguilar	182
Dove Cottage	Alan Sharkey	183
Look up and See…	Shirley Rose	184
A Fool's Message	Leslie Clark Hicks	185
A Maritime Hymn	Joseph Deal	186
Nothing More to Lose	Emile Pinet	187
Bee and Snowdrop	Richard Harries	188
Summer Shine	Neil Mason	189
Mirror of Truth	Archie Papa	189
Water Pearls	Gayle Anne Hart	190
Hats Off	J. Henry DeKnight	190
Dear Mind	Amanda Mtshulana	191

Mood Swings	Terry Bridges	191
4 am	Alan Sharkey	192
Una Vita	Trude Foster	192
Tears from the Sun	Peter Rivers	193
Obsessed	Janette Curran	193
A Decade Passed	Lorna Caizley	194
When Stars they Whisper	Mathew Burgio	194
I Have Walked	J. P. Hayter	195
I Dance with the Darkness	Jennifer M. Nichols	196
Prophecies for the Age…	Michael Hukkanen	197
O, Poetry	Karin J. Hobson	198
Weather	Terry Bridges	199
The Stitch	Joseph Deal	199
The Wild	Anna Treasure	200
The Shadow of Yesterday	Valerie Dohren	201
Under a Different…	Graeme Stokes	202
Tranquility	Simon Drake	203
Promises Broken	Jennifer M. Nichols	204
You're in My Arms	David Catterton Grantz	205
Easyspeak	Gregory Richard Barden	206
For So Long have I Yearned	Linda Adelia Powers	207
Tinea	Trude Foster	208
Night Watch	R. David Fletcher	208
Inversions	Angela Brown	209
Changing Seasons	Donna Smith	210
Love, Not Love	Richard de Bulat	210
No Skeleton is made of Gold	Jessica F. C. Magalhães	211
Pressing Petals	Chuck Porretto	212
Somewhere	John C. Algar	214
Still Emitting Light	Dabendra Sahu	215
you resemble a rapture…	Matt Elmore	216
The Need to Write	Matthew Burgio	217
On this Side of Heaven	Eri Aguilar	218
Gaps in the Sea Wall	Anna Treasure	219
Her Quiet Song	Leslie Clark Hicks	221
Angels for You	W. Fields	222
Angel Babies	Kirsty Howarth	222
The Rage	Taylor Juliet Ashton	223
Final Verse	Jou Wilder	224

Foreword

Wheelsong Poetry Anthology 6 brings together another potent chorus of poetic voices from around the globe. This sixth volume in the acclaimed *Wheelsong Anthology* series features over 260 poems written by 123 emerging and established poets from six continents. Each poem was selected based on its emotional resonance, artistic scope, and shared vision. The review process was rigorous and systematic, so only the best submissions have found their way into this volume.

Curated with care by a dedicated editorial team from across leading online poetry communities—this anthology is more than just a collection of verse. It's a movement. This book is part of a larger mission: to raise both funds and awareness for children living in extreme poverty. In a world overwhelmed by need, our poets offer what they can—*their words*, united together in action.

Proceeds from this book can purchase high-protein sachets that will keep a malnourished child alive for a month. Alternatively, proceeds can purchase two sterile midwifery birthing packs. A little money can go a long way.

Heartfelt, without fear, and globally minded, *Wheelsong Poetry Anthology 6* is firm evidence that poetry not only speaks out the truth—but it also promotes change.

Poetry Against Poverty. That's still who we are.

Steve Wheeler
CEO Wheelsong Books
Founder Invisible Poets
May 2025

Hello
Kevin Francis

In the stillness before dawn
I take up my pen and mourn
Sedentary walks through silence
Assembling the real me
From the wreckage

Festering shame escapes again
A mere inkling takes shape
Ravaging time which ticks in my mind
I hold onto these morose minutes
Like the shallow ledge of a cliff face

Soon the birds will start to sing
Soon the sky will dilute into cerulean
Soon the clouds will become a shroud
Soon there shall be a reflection
Soon I shall have to be me

Wherever I must go I have already been
To hell and back, everywhere in-between
To memories which fall from my mind
Like a coastal erosion, a sudden implosion
Which takes the sleep from my eyes

One last journey for you
Together, we shall go together
And walk once more the drifting sand
And then I shall let you go where you will
Tomorrow I shall be here still
With you.

The Sky
Mieczysław Kasprzyk

The sky, gunmetal grey above,
the ground is damp, the verge alive
with verdant textures, rounded leaves
and pointed spikes. Yellow tulips
against the white camelia.

We never cleared it up, the row,
and now you're ashes anyhow.
We'll never say those closing words
that hovered in the winter air.

And summer'll come, and autumn too,
the clouds will pass, that sky grey-blue.
The seasons flow and time moves on,
all blooms will fade, their glory done.

Time
Brygida Błażewicz

It is we who fall apart in its stillness.
Moments do not pass—
they vanish before you can name them.
What has been becomes a dream within dreams,
and only your body remembers.
Time quivers in an old man's gaze,
in a newborn's first cry,
in the silence between
the words you never spoke.
There is no clock that can save you.
But you can dance
upon the second that still remains.

Weeping Willow
Catherine A. MacKenzie

I rest under a weeping willow,
Watching a darting dragonfly,
A ladybug lands on my shoulder,
Over yonder, a red cardinal chirps,
Earlier I found a polished penny
And days before a velvety feather,
All signs from heaven,
A deceased, delivering love.

Deeper Than Any Blade
Emile Pinet

A poem should be a candle
that brings human feelings to light;
moving like a stubbled shadow
across the face of tomorrow.

And its rhythm should be inviting,
soliciting raw emotions
from within the depths of your soul;
where both Angels and Demons dwell.

Its language should be conversant,
conveying the writer's message
in a relatable fashion;
emotional and personal.

And it should be free of the lies
that ignorance perpetuates;
freeing feelings with wizened words
that cut deeper than any blade.

In Plain Sight
Archie Papa

If we listen very closely as time looks away
wisdom understands what silence can say
bound in the present our minds must stay
the future a dream we'll awaken one day
If kindness lies down as hatred should stand
fate brings the perils which evil has planned
as greed would possess every grain of sand
our joy becomes scant and our sorrow grand
If love finds a way to keep the path clear
a trace of its essence will overcome fear
glimmering memories of those held dear
placed in plain sight of each passing year

My Clay, My Makers
Larry Bailie

That speck of me
This piece of clay
What is water and dust
Now this hardened dried shard
Moulded and shaped
Painted and fired
Softly tuned by the artists
My mother, my father
Missed by us
Loved by us
Allowed me to be me.
Held whole against this day
We are chipped but never broken
Repaired glued like an old dish on a table
Now healing,
they are
Missed by us
Loved by us
Whole again

We Have the Poets
Steve Wheeler

They have the guns
They fire them all day
They have the guns
But we have the poets

They have the bombs
That explode and destroy
They have the bombs
We have the poets

They have the weapons
That injure and maim
They have the weapons
We have the poets

They have the power
They wield it to harm
They have the power
We have the poets

They will wage war
But they'll never win
Because we have the poets
Yes, we have the poets

Sunburst
Sarah Sansbury

On the winter shore
a sunburst in the slate sky
banana-yellow
single kite proudly soaring
defiantly shouting joy

Burning Memories
Karen Bessette

The burning memories of you
etched in my heart and soul
under a cold, abrasive bitter sky.

The Soul of a Poet
W. Fields

take the reins in my dreams…
while I'm sleeping and awake
on restless nights I pray my soul for you to overtake
guide my mouth when strayed away
from thresholds to my heart
and bless this tongue to muster words…
which validates my art

I'll usher signs of astonishment
spewing lines from centuries past
and make your body marvel
as I induct future amassed
and we'll savor what I'll conjure
In the present to your being
as I summon from my prose a calm
that's seldom felt or seen

for I am the fountain, I am the wave,
I am the mountain which fosters the brave
I am the thermostat where temperatures set
forging the climate with no regret

the soul of a poet spawns perpetual seeds
to the spirits of which they are sewn
as the water breeds life and the life gives breath
we will soar to heights unknown

In 50 Years
Natasha Browne

Oh, to roll on 50 years,
I would be eighty-eight,
I wonder how my fate,
Would take its toll.

I would love to grow old,
But instead,
Of a futuristic future,
I would love if we returned to innocence.

All repent,
Break down the fence,
Live,
Give back to the land,
Understand,
Where we came from,
Remember our ancestors who have gone.

Live on,
Be strong,
Have no wars,
Visit our shores,
Have cleaner oceans,
Where everyone shares devotion,
To each other,
I hope to be a mother,
Then a grandmother.

I'd cover,
The world in flowers,
Let them grow during the showers,
I'd spend hours,
Sitting on a porch,
In a rocking chair,
In the night air.

Reading and writing poetry still,
Have a little book shelf on my window sill,

I'd be old and grey,
Be grateful to everyone who stayed,
In my life the last fifty years.
I'd face my fears,
Of being old,
Breaking moulds.

I'd have a little vegetable patch,
I'd laugh,
Across my old frail face,
I'd be moving at a slower pace,
But have more grace.

There will be no wars,
No politics,
Everyone would live out in the sticks.

No large cities,
But forests so pretty,
We'd discover ourselves,
There would be no cells,
Just spells,
Of better summers,
I'd sit on my porch,
Greet all the runners.

In fifty years,
There would be no competition,
But everyone in the perfect career,
That suits only them,
When,
We are fifty years plus,
We'd not make a fuss,
But still pray,
Ask God to stay.

But, for now,
At Thirty-eight,
I can wait,
To grow fifty years older,
Forever this way,
I would stay.

Night Waits
Linda Adelia Powers

Rising to salute the twilight
      grateful again you have come home
         able to breathe light in the dark
   try sleep in your arms until dawn

Dreams rehearse the raw shock of betrayal
      replay the freeze of your leaving again
         grinding teeth can't cut through
   sinews of fear tightening the lungs

Shards of trust broken cycle the bloodstream
      cut rest with nameless fair faces
         here's the silently screaming scene
   the reawakening to consciousness jolted

Morning harkens again nightmare darkened
      hugs pretend ghosts are banished
         goodbyes suspend the haunting
   while night waits to redeliver the heartache

The Burning Truth
Ashly Tenini

You spoke of love with a silver tongue,
But truth was twisted, sharp and young.
I wore your blame like a second skin,
A quiet ache that burned within.

You lit the match and watched me burn—
But flames don't plead; they scorch and churn.
From ash, I rose with nothing to prove—
A truth too fierce for you to remove.

Stolen Words
Sarah Jane Holden

Stolen words leave broken hearts,
Broken hearts lead to empty pages,
Empty pages mean limited stories,
Limited stories create constraints,
Constraints means no full stories,
No full stories due to stolen words.

God's Garden
Gregory Richard Barden

of all the dear intents that I'm shaped of
    no grand pursuit's more critical than love—
        while all the world about me comes apart
   I'm but the soil for Heaven's hope, above

this life has pushed me often to a seam
    the fringe of hell to see a gloried scheme
        and though it oft' was of my own device
   God used each conflict to define a dream

that tho' life's issues have a varied range
    and some may press the definition strange
        the truest resolution through God's grace—
  it's love alone accomplishes true change

tho' it might seem too simple at the start
    the scripture that defines me does impart
        one single truth has been and yet shall be—
  'tis *love* the seed God's sowing in my heart.

Empty Spaces
David Cragg

The stars at night seem lonely
But it is the empty space between
That makes them beautiful

Burned in a Dream
Nadia Martelli

Tomorrow's dawn
With all its blurred promises,
Rises from the darkness,
Eroding black betrayal
With a sublime smile,
A relief from the inky shadows
Of insomnia and obscure needs,
Words that crumble in their elegy
To wars and all the waste, there,
Where the scorched eye of day
Consumes all resistance
To the heat of the score…
The lost direction, of which route
To stumble along, before my step
Trips and falls into the void
Of unknown Hope
And off-line substance, listening
To bones creeping towards a cure,
Looking for the purest spell
To cast in the dust;
My ballad's blue-black tune
Is stuck, as it ponders
Upon the day's adjournments,
Burned in a dream…

Fragility of Being
Michael Hukkanen

Broken fingers
weave
sudden Angels
from the bones
of autumn nights
where cricket songs
endure
the fragility of being
All the stars have teeth
in the open mouth
of the sky
and winter is grumbling
with hunger

Freeze Frame
Tracy Taylor

Fast forward
pause
rewind
Repeat the images
over and over and over
until I cannot breathe
unable to find what's wrong
what's right
what's imagined
what's real
My heart thuds on the
freeze of one frame

The Bridge I Trace
Jodeci Flores

I've seen it in the arches of old cities,
where stone curves like a held breath,
a quiet defiance against time.
Bridges not just for crossing,
but for carrying the weight of empires.
How something so enduring
can bend so gracefully
is a mystery I long to solve.

And the cypress, tall and deliberate,
its spine a ridge drawn by the hand of eternity,
leaning, but never breaking.
The shadow sways with a rustling hymn,
a testament to roots unseen.
Your elegance is there too,
rising without effort,
like it was always meant to be.

The dhow sails across my thoughts,
its prow slicing through amber waters,
a vessel of mahogany,
shaped by patience and devotion,
born of craftsmen who listened to the sea.
It tilts toward the horizon,
a frame of measured poise,
etched with the promise of return.

And now, as sleep gathers you,
I trace the slope of your nose,
its arc a hymn to arches unseen.
Each line I follow draws me closer,
like bridges, trees, and sails
were always destined to bring me here,
to this sacred, tender embrace,
with my hand caressing your face.

Wonder in Our Hearts
Larry Bailie

On to hike into the mountain's beauty
Watching the turn of the sun overhead
Your madness has reason for now you duty
To find a suitable place to set camp
If you have ever been here
You are a friend of mine
Standing ankle deep in a mountain lake
And wonder about your sanity
Feeling the water crisp and cold
Ready to jump head first, leaving humanity
That suck of air is not so rare
If you have been here
You are a friend of mine
Watching the ram standing
on a rail thin ledge
Your hands clasp each elbow
holding yourself seeing this wonder
If you have been here
You are a friend of mine
Backing up to a cook fire
As sun breaks the crust of the world
The scent is smoky morning breakfast
If you ever been here
You are a friends of mine
My friend is lying, while others praying
and from my pocket the photo
of us
Gazing at an open valley
Taken by a passer by
I Place it in your hands
Saying we have been here
You are a friend to mine

The Beach
D. A. Simpson

the beach looked so beautiful that night
hauntingly beautiful like a painting
and possessed of a dream like quality
as a thin vapour tinged with a soft purple
hovered over the scene

when the sun went down
affecting its slow descent
upon a canvas of lilacs and lavenders
mixed with swatches of salmon pink
and buttercup yellows
the tableau to embellish

and the sea hissed on the sand
sucking at the shoreline
a'stirring and a'sifting
each golden grain,
pale now in the spectral light

as wave after wave retreated
into the impenetrable darkness
pervading the benthic realm of midnight blue

and lapped at the hem of the shore
forming a creamy white froth
that sparkled at the water's edge
in the ethereal glow
emitted by a serene dusk

while a far horizon brooded in indigo
at the foothills of the crepuscular heavens
aloft in an endless cosmos
and a silent breeze wafted
across the deserted expanse

Leeward
Shirley Rose

A small Western town squats in the lee
Of the neighboring mountain that hovers
Over their roofs and back yards, protecting
Them from storms and prevailing winds
Clouds and threats of snow pass over them
Quickly, moving on to farther more wide-open
Spaces

A tiny sailing vessel finds a squall, follows the lee
Of the blow until it reaches shallower, calmer water
Arriving dockside, beach side, safe and sound
From torn sails, broken rudder, smashed bow
Compromised hull, drowned passengers, blue
Faces

A homeless person in a metropolis sits in the lee
Of a skyscraper, taking advantage of the shade
And shadow, the shield and safety of the height
The strength of brick and block, concrete, rock
Even tempered glass. The warming sun can't reach
Down into the shadowed canyons, alleyways of
hopelessness
But the blizzards and blasts of snow and rain,
Deflected

A woman, small in stature, defenceless against
Violence or crime, even hateful words or incrimination
Will look for a man with a tall, deep chest
Strong and broad shoulders, stiff neck, long arms
Powerful back to protect and defend her against
Any attacker, any storm, any foe, any blow, she
Will look for a man to travel with, stand in his lee
Protected

The Sleeper in the Vale
Robert Atkins

A patch of greenery, a river sings and glides:
It madly sews its threads to grasses—fabrics gay
In silver; here the sun from lofty mountain's pride
Shines: a hidden valley frothing with the rays.

A little soldier boy lies open-mouthed, no cap,
He bathes his weary neck in fresh and bluish cress,
How pale he is in sleep—the clouds around him wrap:
Tucked in a bed of green the rains of sunlight bless.

His feet lie in a group of gladioli, sleep
Has soothed this invalid and made him smile in deep
Peace; O Nature warm him, for the child is cold.

The perfumes pass him by—no odours stir his rest,
He sleeps beneath the sun, his hand upon his breast
Unmoving. He bears in his right side two red holes.

Inviting Waters
Charlene Phare

Ripples lay calm, shades are cast
Spearmint dreams now diminished
Inviting waters calling your name
Life's double edged sword, thinnest
Elongated thoughts weathered
Past that remains still chequered

Daggers drawn from mighty stone
Chartered flights take to the skies
Multiplying scars are cloned
Devils anguish in disguise
Rivers continue running deep
Invited waters gently creep

Summers Sojourns
Tanya Raval

Summers Sunbird sucking, succulent species in the sun,
Earth an enchanting essence, an enigma of an escalating burn,
Bees buzzing with bewildered butterflies basking in the sun,
Being blind to the thermal throttle to an upward turn,
Flowers frolic fragrance from far,
Formed for love, fathom from afar,
Animals attain another aplomb with an open door ajar,
Mating more and more merrily, masking meaning of life a dance,
Moon and sun swoon and saunter their sojourns just by chance,
Life a living love affair, looking lovely forever fair,
Dance dear devotee devout,
In Lord's land, living life without doubt.

Patchwork
Kendra Bower

I do not understand why it is, that I do what I do
why this compulsion to scribble words
on scraps of paper
and years later have these obscure scrawls
turn up in dresser drawers
you tilt your head and search the coffee stains
it must mean something
life becomes this patchwork—
twenty thirty forty years of broken verse
it must be more than random firing of neurons
in Truth, we never capture Beauty
She is wild and without Form
but one morning I saw a hawk learn to fly
and a salmon the size of the canoe!

The Golden Ribbons of the World
Victoria Puckering

Through the golden ribbons of the world
The inked words ride on their flimsy tails
As human voices converse in the subtle breeze
Poetry is lived and deeply breathed
Travelling across wild oceans and seas
Catching the purist diamonds in the darkest velvet sky
Two beating ruby hearts
Glancing at the same changing skies
Across many different timelines
Where human touch, can never be defined
As I write my next inked line
A verse, so divine …

Decline and Fall
Terry Bridges

Old age's magnificent loneliness empowers me
Screams me into writing this attempt at autobiographical art
Dates are as uncertain as days in my finite existence
What events I remember howl like banshees in the night
I tenderly tiptoe through the long dark hours warily
Burst through caustic clouds to a dawn-like revolution
My hopes stirred in a pot...a witch's cauldron of sour emotions
A strange brew fortified nourishing that pleases me
I visit this hell of an adventure holiday regularly to top up
Battering my cracked heart against fortune's fickle fate
What can I tell you of civilisation's foretold sorry collapse?
Only that I was there experiencing the light diminishing at the end

A Raven
Brygida Błażewicz

a raven sat at the edge of day
as if it knew
something was ending

it didn't caw
didn't stare
it simply was
a black comma
between light and shadow

a second fell from the sky
quiet as a thought
that cannot be spoken

their presence
carried no fear
only silence
deep as earth after rain

and then I understood
they are signs
for those who see beyond

Inner Storm
Rose Marie Streeter

Destiny unknown
as 'morrows leap
into oblivion
where havoc demands
full attention
holding captive
my soul
    in realms
        of despair...

Practical Physics
Steve Wheeler

I don't want to swing on a star.
My hands would be badly burnt;
also, the vacuum of space
is a dangerous playground.

I don't want to carry any
moonbeams home in a jar.
Photons cannot be captured
inside a glass receptacle.

The entire project would be
doomed from the start
just like the hope of any
lasting romance with you.

Bluster will Blister
Kwaku Adjei-Fobi

Bluster will blister,
and we will pick up empty cocoons
out of the vain catacombs

Bombast will not last
beyond the flowers' blooms,
and floated reality will evolve into kapok.

Bravado basks in brevity
for the lights and the cameras mere.
The facades wear off,
fantastically fizzled.

Accumulation
Tom Cleary

As I lie recumbent
I find the measure of a cumulus
the contour of each curl
the width of its wisps
and traces of its tails
unlimited
just as when I look up at you
I'm unable to count
let alone label
the length and depth
in all the ways you love me.

I am your sky
but you are my sun.

It never did Me no Harm
Richard de Bulat

Didn't have a label, when I was a lad,
There just weren't enough to go round,
And it's not that I didn't have problems,
It's just that a beating was sound.

Whether policemen were clipping your ear,
Or a teacher caning your palm,
Whatever I did, I got a good wallop,
But it never did me no harm.

So what that I twitch at hearing loud noise,
Have a permanent tick in both arms,
I can't function each day without drinking,
It just never did me no harm....

No, it never did me no harm

Are You ...
Tom Watkins

Are you drunk the text inquired
I responded, no, not in the moment
In the moment I am a poet

Ah, the series of messages
on my phone probed

Are you hurt?
My reply, I am a poet

Are you lonely?
I am a poet

Are you sad?
I am a poet

Wallowing in grief?
I am a poet

Are you OK?
I am a poet

Seemingly they wanted
to find something "wrong"
All is okay
I view life as a continuum
with both pain and joy
with neither hanging around forever

Then they got to the heart of the matter
by asking the tougher question,
Are you a poet?

I am hurt, sad, angry, perplexed, alone and
lonely at times
I experience pain both real and imagined

Also....
I find joy and happiness
and wake each morning grateful
that I remain alive ready to absorb my life
For my own edifications,
with a compelling need to feel alive

I choose to express
my emotions and feelings
in the moment in words
I would sculpt, draw or paint if I was able
I am not talented in that way
Through expression I feel

When I experience
the symphony of emotions
I know I am still alive
It is why I like to cry

If my imagination and written feelings create
an aesthetic spark in others
I hope it enhances
your sense of being

It also makes me feel joyful,
happy and alive

Am I?
I am

My Neurodivergent Brain
Iain Strachan

Quantum tunnelling between rabbit holes
This uncertain mind of mine
Finds deep connections
Where random thoughts jazz and jam
And my divergent Muse
Sometimes makes a metaphor that hits
And sometimes dribbles drivel and gibberish.

And sometimes, I'm drawn into Autism's vortex
When I hear you but don't listen
When I see you but can't read you,
When, fixated in a pit of special interest
My brain tries to fit fragmented bits
Into the music of verse whose rhythm fits.

Or maybe in rapt contemplation
Of curious numbers like a hundred and thirty one
Trying to decipher its meaning:
Could it be a granitic palindromic prime?
Or should it be construed as a different story
Like ten squared plus two to the fifth less one?
Then the austere dance of numbers holds me
That absolute truth of maths enfolds me.

So when I say something bizarre,
when you can't see the connection,
when the conversation's context
has long since changed
and it's no longer germane,
that's when I have to explain:
it's just my neurodivergent brain.

Feeling of Exile
Famara S. Sock

Sitting on the white sand by the sea on a Sunday.
Surrounded by a crowd that was loud and lively.
Suddenly a deep feeling of emptiness hit me.
I felt like a fish, in the middle of a desert.

Somewhere in-between
Hayley Sejberg

Hell is where the heart is
The devil would say
Hell is where you can't wash your sins away
Listen to the sirens
On repeat all day
Here you will feel the pain
For the rest of your days
Heaven is where the heart is
The angels would say
Here you can wash away
Your sins with forgiveness
As god is your witness
One step forward
Don't look back
Move towards the light
Keep focused on holding the good in sight
Once a portal opened in time
Alarmingly noisy and shining bright
A voice it called my name so clear
Loud and masculine
I stood still
The ground it moved
I came to my knees
What would have happened if I had gone in?
Would it be heaven or hell
Or somewhere in-between

Grains of Dust
D. A. Simpson

grains of dust a myriad
toward the floor a'drifting,
caught in a beam of light
cast by the orb of day
into the cleat bursting

a mirage of a millions drops of gold
flooding the somnolent scene
at the very duskhour

bathed in hues of saffron and tangerine

and a pale sun hung low
at the hem of the tranquil celestial sheet
nudging above the water's edge

waiting awhile

it bore a thin aura in the cool air
that pervaded the encroaching evenfall

and was reflected upon the limpid surface
exulting atop the benthic deep of indigo blue

while an insubstantial mist,
insubstantial as a breath
began to form
dimming the glow emanating
from the monarch of midnight

as dreams began to bestir
within the minds
of the silently slumbering

Daddy's Little Girl
Larry Bracey

Why am I so nervous,
We always knew this day would come,
You'd walk me down the aisle,
Why do I feel so numb,

I feel like when you do,
Your little girl will be no more,
Trading her teddy bear for a townhouse,
And that room I grew up in,
you'll just ignore,

All the things I left behind,
I promise I'll come and get,
Call me to remind me,
You know I'm going to forget,
Kiss mom on the forehead,
Every single day,
Take her mind off missing me,
By assuring her I'll be okay,
Thank you dad, for everything,
Now let's go get this done,
If you start to cry, I'll cry,
It'll be in front of everyone,

So wipe away your tears,
Stand up straight, and be strong,
Give your girl one last hug,
Before they play our song.

We are Not the Broken Things...
Zac Warden

The wind of change sings,
Of the broken things,
Oh, How to some it must haunt.
Blasphemy, within inclusive harmony,
Your narrow borders it will taunt.
The disenfranchised, or
those the other side of the track.
A community of continuity,
Accepting of all, that polite society may still lack.
Beige ever whinges,
Of the outer fringes.
Where they sport a different hue.
Both parties confused,
By that they peruse.
Who's observing who at the zoo?
Hiding in plain sight,
The non-contrite,
Forming their own tribes.
The self-identifiers,
No longer outsiders,
Alongside supporting scribes.
Souls of the not quite,
Dancing in the solstice light.
Ridiculed by those comfortable in the rain.
Creatures of the night,
by dawn giving flight,
To hide from the sun their pain.
More and more subscribers,
To the ranks of the outsiders.
Until who is different is no longer clear.

Fluid acceptance of all
Allowing all to stand tall,
Until to be queer is no longer queer.
Opinions reverse, upon the neural-diverse.
The shadows will constrain no more.

Now with light on their face,
Previous censure a disgrace,
Hear their righteous roar!
For all those once labelled broken,
now self re-assembled,
there is beauty in their scars.
For I see not uniform rows of brilliance,
When I look up, upon the stars.
No, for we are loud, we are proud,
for we have come, so very far.
You see, we never were the broken,
We are but, who we are…

Wren
James Alexander Crown

Flutters of tiny wings
Are seen,
Amongst the trees and bushes green,
'Tis a sin to kill a wren they say,
Save in Ireland
On Saint Stephen's Day.

For Saint Stephen
Did the wren betray,
Or so the learnèd scholars say.
The saint pursued by wicked men,
Their gaze drawn in by the frolicsome wren.

Drawn in towards his hiding place,
Where hid the saint all full of grace.

The Saint a martyr thus became,
The sons of Ireland lay the blame
Upon the tiny wren, the same
Who made a martyr
So they claim.

Hungry Lullaby
Ryan Morgan

Take this briar bowl.
Quaff from it quick.

It's not fairy broth.
It's not fairy broth.

It will seal the teeth
In your belly's maw,
And then you can sleep.
And then you can sleep.
Take this stony plate
And swiftly eat.

It's not pixie bread.
It's not pixie bread.

And the hunger within
Shall be spurned again,
So you can sleep.
So you can sleep.
Take this thorny cup.
Trust and sup.

It is my love.
It is my love.

In this hollow world
It's all I have

To ease you to sleep.
To ease you to sleep.

Alchemystical
Scot A. Buffington

Romancing gold from sugared lead
no alchemist has ever made
love incantations left unsaid
well-ionized before decayed.

No crystal vial may love constrain
nor gilded brass of false pretence
may formulate nor keep contained
hearted plasmas, self-defence.

Confounded chemists quest for fire
created math and recipes
no logic quantifies desire
and baffles claims of remedies.

Affections void all science known
atomic weights can't measure souls
nor bonds covalent stitched and sewn
may twine one mind, disparate wholes.

Quantum entanglements are real
as kisses felt blown into space
defying physics to reveal
the lip imprints upon the face.

Two adorations equal fall
aligned in mass and gravity
the magnetism's protocol
fulfils a heart's concavity

Not all life shoots straight from stars
ghosts compound their own design
two lovers mate their avatars
exist as gifts they made divine.

Poetically Country
Rose Marie Streeter

Chipmunks scurry
to and fro...
play tag
in rustling
leaves...
squirrels
chitter chatter
leap from
tree to tree

close by
in a
babbling brook...
ducks wade
their way
downstream...
babies stagger
close to mom
with freedom
just to be

flowers dressed
in pretty gowns
velvety 'n soft...
each pirouette
one by one
to sounds of
nature songs

attention drawn
to critters
leapfrogging
on a log...
tiny lizard
hitches ride...

turtle
tags along

butterflies
flutter past
land on
crimson rose…
stir aromatic
pleasure
teasing, tickles
nose

poetically country
dreaming
sweet smells…
sights…
and sounds…
gardens
of serenity…
keeps inner
    being strong…

Ode to Us
Anna Treasure

They say there's no
sound in space,
but this blue marble
thrums with song.

The trees, the grasses,
coke cans and door jambs
are played by the wind.
Rocks pound
in the river,

providing bass.

While dogs and foxes bark
the ants click their
jaws, cracking seeds.
The gecko chortles and
my fingers tap on the keys
as I write about us.
These poems
are our song.
The words we
scratch and tap
and the sounds
they make are our
barks, warbles and meows.
This is where the rubber
hits the road.

Some words are
as round
as a stone,
others spiky
with indignation.
The flighty,
the passionate,
the flinty, the solid,
the fillers of space,
the evocative
on-a-mat-op-oeiaic
elegiac,
swirling curling
words just

life effervescing.

Once More
Archie Papa

All that we pretend to be
masks adorned for all to see
thick and thin, one by one
shown to each and everyone
All these layers take their toll
bearing on the heart and soul
shadows cast in fear and doubt
blur the insight looking out
In simple light the truth we see
through a lie's opacity
all that's true within the core
will shed the layers clean once more

A Photo of You
Richard de Bulat

Your photograph, a composed formulation
Of shape and structure, the light and the dark
That makes this picture unique, reality.

Is it an emotion, that a print of you
evokes; some feeling that's inside oneself,
Over a life placed under glass in a frame.

A picture of you, when young, old, or with kids,
I've taken few over so many years,
The charisma of your eyes, in every stare.

The window to your soul, or mine, in a flash,
A reflected arc of retinal light,
In a snapshot moment, that's outlasting time,

Fixed eternally in trenchant black and white.

Gift
R. David Fletcher

Shattered lands, impoverished children,
Crying across time and generations,
Poets' songs sing out to them,
Across our seas and warring nations.
They mobilize with hearts on sleeve,
To reach small souls to love and feed,
Nourish minds and bodies to achieve,
Gift to the beautiful child in need.

My Soul
J. P. Hayter

Oh my soul wants to sing!
See the richness that's in everything!
Oh fly like a bird,
Isis cries,
Her grief stricken heart,
The falcon flies,
Eye of Horus
Searches the landscape,
Its freedom only tethered by Osiris's sighs!
Scattered in the arid landscapes,
Oh my soul wants to sing!
And my heart is everything!
Scattered pieces
Follow the falcons eyes,
It knows in each moment where sorrow lies!
And so my soul wants to sing!
To see there's magic in everything!

Tonight
Karen Bessette

There are no stars
out tonight,
no lovers anywhere,
just one lonely soul
praying to the moody
crying moon.

Unseen
Roger Simpson

At least, not noticed
Buried in the detail
Nature's small print
Infinitesimally minuscule
Is it there or not
Where is it, and when
Inferred rather than observed
Probable, then
Rather than certain
Found in data
That insubstantial medium
Of notional patterns
And obscure mathematics
So, reasonably likely
It is somewhere
At least at some point
And may be again
Theoretically
So we look again
For the fundamentals
Beyond vision
Into the abstraction
Of thought

Ubiquitous
Lorna McLaren

I am the dust upon the wind that blows,
the dark against the candle glow,
the whisper on the Autumn breeze,
the bite that comes with Winter's freeze.
I am the thoughts that lurk inside your head,
the words you wish you'd never said,
the cry of sorrow no-one will hear,
the loneliness that comes with fear.
I am the smile that forms upon your lips,
the remembrance of that first sweet kiss,
the wonder of what Spring regains,
the laughter in the Summer rains.
I am the sadness of a broken dream,
I'm all the things you've never been,
I am everything you'll ever miss,
I'm all around … ubiquitous.

A Single Word
Michael Hukkanen

my brain is covered in folds
where I like to hide, sometimes
I draw the curtains, let the light in,
peek outside where it is noisy,
full of traffic and advertising
Everything is for sale, out there
but no one can afford a heart
Inside I have a chest of drawers
filled with a thousand words for
sorrow and, spelled in silent letters,
a single word for love

the look before my leap
Matt Elmore

my expression betrays my mystique
deep feelings left secret, I keep inside
do you see the look before my leap?
on the very edge, at this very peak
immense emotions I seek to hide
my expression betrays my mystique
a long way down to up the creek
I release tears of joy, subside my pride
do you see the look before my leap?
when I get mad, I feel the heat
or dare to grieve; I can't deny
my expression betrays my mystique
I'm only human, I'm no freak
yet there is a rugged wall I hide behind
do you see the look before my leap?
so this is the moment I must meet
up to the breach, I smile and sigh
my expression betrays my mystique
do you see the look before my leap?

Hope's Shadow
Martha M. Miller

Despair is the darkest shadow
tethered to the feather
perched in silence and grasping notes
waiting for bad weather
For when the gale wings start to squall
a rain of tears will fall
stealing that tiny bird's sweet song
mocking the ebb and loss
The feather may be swept away
drowned in the raging sea
but storms do dissipate
and doves have more feathers to sing

Through their Gaze
Ashly Tenini

If love were a dog, it would be heaven on earth,
A heartbeat of purity, a life filled with worth.
Unwavering eyes that mirror my soul,
A love without limits, steadfast and whole.

If hate had a face, it would mirror mankind,
A shadow of cruelty, selfish and blind.
The innocent suffer at careless hands,
And yet their loyalty still withstands.

My dogs are my children, my bridge to grace,
A fleeting warmth in time's cruel chase.
To me, they are threads in the life I weave—
To them, I am all things—world, breath, belief.

I see God in their gaze, the divine in their trust,
A love that won't fade, though bodies turn to dust.
Love whispers and stays, though time pulls it thin,
Yet the world betrays them, again and again.

Cruelty should never find its place,
Yet it lingers on, a disgusting disgrace.
I will stand alone, even if the world turns its back,
While you drown in your greed, in the lies you can't track.

A crowd of hatred, pity dressed as spite,
Jealousy coiling, dimming the light.
A thirst for power, a need to command,
While compassion is buried in the sinking sand.

If love were a dog, then love would be me,
For theirs is the world that I long to see.

A Lovers' Tiff
Stephen James Smith

After our argument
Did you really think
I would just sit here
Like a mourner
Listening to the slow
Ticking hands
Of the clock
Bellowing out
Lost love
Like battering ballads?
Or did you think
I would wander
This new world
Like a traveller lost
In the desolate
Desert of death
Drowning in salt tears
Thirsting for your love?
Well, I am not!
I am not jumping
Off the cliff edge
Of my mind,
I am not wearing
An obsidian rock face
Of mourning
Tweezing
Spears of splinters
From my blistered heart.

And what are you now?

Just a forgotten memory
Like salty sea dust
Dead and buried
In the sands of the past.
Please come back, I was only joking!

Echoes
Kendra Bower

once I met a Persian poet on the way to the airport
they spoke fiercely of love and death and God

I remember their passion and their conviction

I remember it with panther precision
that feeling of being shattered and stitched
that feeling of being transformed and transfixed
that moment echoes in me still
we preamble through the world
shedding moments like skin
with a wink and a smile and a Cheshire grin
all the days and nights we spent
your echo should be shimmering sea glass;
a pool filled with magical fish
instead its painted black; a pure abyss
save for the Baltic Gold around your eyes
sealing the Judas Kiss I left you with

I tried to use my pain for good
I witnessed more than I probably should
I sat in silence while tales were told
I brewed the tea and waited
watched as you carefully undressed
until I saw the naked truth, your soul stripped bare

I hope you remember that someone was there
those stories echo in me still
if we must become broken in order to be light
perhaps I will survive the weighing of the heart
when I lay myself down to sleep,

I hope yours is the echo I get to keep

My Love for Freedom
Rafik Romdhani

We share the morning coffees
and night's warm blankets.

We hearken to butterflies
and pavilion-like foliage.
Each of us would have a role.

Mine was to feed the pigeons
from the white bags of wheat
before I take them to the mill
and have them ground.

Pigeons should eat
before anyone else,
like revered queens.

I was selfish enough,
but my love for freedom
continues to gnaw at my ribs.

I ferry unfinished dreams to the moon.
and madly dance with the face of dawn,
with all the toys that once deserted me.

We share the morning coffees
and night's warm blankets.
We share the first cactus rose
and run after the ghosts born
from the ripped womb of dust.

We sit in front of bleak houses,
facing the fields of oblivion.
We share coffins on our shoulders,
and moans beneath bricks and stones.

She Dreams
Michelle Tarbin

One day she dreams of delivering such rapturous rhythms and rhymes—a poem worthy of clicky fingers, ecstatically elicited from sublime, poetic perfection.

Her mind doesn't trickle like a slow flowing river, it churns like rushing waterfalls and hits like an avalanche of prose prised from the depths of her heart.

She feels herself shrink like Alice in Wonderland, growing small in long shadows cast by gargantuan giants of such graceful beauty, wielded by the power of their pen, these wordsmiths, oh my.

The majesty of their mountainous talent so great she'd not reach the first summit to plant that flag, cross the horizon to open the door in her mind to allow the words to flow out.

Lost in a quagmire of self-doubt, struggling to compete with such Goliath abilities and skill, her hand paled in insignificance—unable to speak; Instead growing curious she sought how to learn—grow—by process of osmosis learning from their greatness.

She dreams of producing such poetic melodies, muddled together from a life lived in Technicolor—subdued, now in black and white, silenced by breath stolen from Covid's curse. Elegance escapes her grasp replaced by shards of glass, words stuck deep in her throat barely spoke but spat out in rage at her condition.

The complexities of these expert wordsmiths weaving rhythms and rhymes like magicians leaves her paltry offerings begging 'I'm not enough.' How can she compete with these lyrical feats when she can barely stand on her own poetic left feet.

Twisting and turning, thrashing and churning yearning—she can't sleep—nor can she write that last verse.

Should she give up, turn away, cry, despise her lack of creative ability, unable to comply to what is required to shine in this sky full of stars or shall she make one last stand;

—a battle cry—from this humble poetic pilgrim, one last stab in the darkness of space to create something beautiful to leave behind in this world filled with darkness and light—

Poetic love shall conquer all, and all will be forgiven.

Endless Breath
Karin J. Hobson

Across realms of Citrine fields
and robustly lush emerald greens;
Over endless rolling hills amaze to
venturous strays by distant streams;
Satiated rippling seas of Buttercup frills,
doting wand whetting sun-filled spills,
Coaxing heart's thrill by trill; Oh, lure of
canvas-white for want of colours will!
~
Gulps of cool morn air, swigs by swills affair
quenching orbs, bountiful stares, aware;
Extended arms, lustful gaze, indulging,
jubilance by glorious praise!
Wander, wander, what wading wafting whiffs
from lilac sprigs to given saunters!
Where dainty drip-drops of dewy wet mist
rest in gist upon the satin red rose petal's lip
~
Baptismal barters on glory's sweet display,
validating vintage glint of golden Sun-rays;
I hear thrilling trills of a lone whippoorwill,
and know this to be my last breath fulfilled.

Jealousy Station
Peter Rivers

This is a futuristic far
from holistic modern age at hand
Ads everywhere a megaphone
for the haves and the have nots
But wait for a second people,
then they say it steals joy to compare…
Sure as the driven snow would know,
we don't get very far with an empty car
So off we go scuttle and scurry
to seedy stores called convenience

We pull up to fill up each and every day
Ding ding
Top it off would ya!
Archaic old pump station pumps
from a simpler time
Hmm, isn't that odd now?
That isn't gas on that sign….
It's liquid jealousy
We fill our tanks with that fuel
all the way anyway
Then drive away…

Fast forward countless dreadful years;
Everyone racing spewing
poisonous toxic fumes of survival
Genuine love for everyone
needs a serious grass roots revival
What I feel is more like walking death row,
from trial to trial
Why does being gracious and thankful seem
as if it's gone out of style?
I wonder what world we'd see
if each and every day
we tried it for a while…

Man
W. Fields

the grateful recipient of life
I'm told that I'm made from clay
a powerful breath from the omnipotent creator...
charted me on my way

the pathway of choice is before me
and a foe to besmirch my good name
the taunting accuser wields taskmaster's whip
and my suffering, part of his game

but his venue and venture to register fear...
will cease function with a wickedness band
as light from an armor
that embodies my spirit...
ignites true intentions for man

I have power to give life and take it away..
as the former aligns with my soul
and yet the inhabited powers to be
bears false witness from depths of Shaol

but on the path my shoulders are broadened
bequeathing tenacity to all...
who cultivate seeds from the Blood of the Deity..
which enlightens all who may call

I stride arm in arm with the Angels
as they hoist me to plateaus unknown
when dispatched, the *Spirit* through a summoning tongue,
unleashes them straight from *God's* throne

life's valleys, hills and mountains
doth not liken to quickening sand
for the plight, the sweat,
the blood and the struggle
are purposed...
to heighten a Man

Chosen
Alan Sharkey

How long will that last?
That gushing torrent of love.
That burning desire to watch you succeed,
a lifetime of course
A lifetime of yearning,
Of heartache and pain
So immeasurable and eternal
It's pure, yet such joy
I see you, I feel you, we are one
And yet worlds apart
The inspiration, the learning
You are my teacher, my orb
Grow, and conquer your world
Fill it with beauty and knowledge.
Expand your inner gods
And destroy your demons
This is yours, take it
Take it to new levels and remember
You are loved and you are here
And I will always be here with you
How long will that last?
A lifetime of course
For I am you and you are me
We are the same, we are chosen

Love
Melissa Stegall

Love has no finder's fee
Love opens up early, you can
catch it on sale, it's *free*.
Love is special, if you just
look out, can't you see?
Love is you and me.

No Words
Tracy Taylor

Backstage chatter
break a leg
you've got this
enjoy every moment
Pointe shoes in the rosin box
scraping and grinding
bun too tight
stage makeup
drying and cracking
Lights up
curtains up
deep breaths
and butterflies

There will be no words
on this stage
I speak in
exuberant grand jetés
perfectly executed fouettées
and pirouettes
intricate entrechats
and languorous renversés
Perfect legs and turnout
gorgeously pointed feet
fluttering arms
and delicate hands

I need no words
to speak with my audience

In the Palm of My Hand
Fouzia Sheikh

In the Palm of my hand
I hold a future
A future to unfold
A world of stories
in a single line.

In the palm of my hand
I hold a dream
With the promise
of an untold tale
and an unseen sight.

In the palm of my hand
I hold a life,
A life waiting to happen.
all down the road.

In the palm of my hand
I hold my heart
Cradle it gently, my love
So it will never fall apart.

In the palm of my hand
I hold myself
A warrior alive to fight

Myself
I will not be broken.

Ore
Corey Reynolds

It's hard for you to know
I am now made of wood mostly
also fire and blood
not steel stone or urban ore
these were the materials at hand
I can be damaged and repaired
I can make you sing and cry and laugh
we share ourselves and our burning timbre
we run headlong like lake swimmers
to drink our fill and vanquish the little things
to quench the heat of anger
turning those old things to something touchable
charring these warm days into ashen
starlit nights to look at and forget
traveling not far meandering near nightlights
moths that flutter around the streetlights
like creatures that don't exist
between the bars lit up sign and the hard
dirt and ore

Until the River Ends
Dale Parsons

We will follow the eternal river
Just two tiny white specks amid vivid, vibrant colour
Flanked by trees with their bright and lavish leaves
We will go where the river leads
To where the river flows, we will follow
Wander deep blue waters, under pale blue skies
Through tetrachromatic eyes, I see the brightest swan
And I will follow loyally…forever-long
We will ride the ripples forever
No tie nor tether, two tiny specks of pure white feather
Just you and me, you see, swans they stay together
I will follow you my friend, until the eternal river ends

I'll Water Your Flowers
Mike Rose

Late at night
Is when I need you the most
So I'll come walking in
Like a long grieving ghost

When I lay down on the dirt
We're going to talk for hours
And right before I leave
I'll water your flowers

I'll show you some pictures
And talk about the new calf
Then tell you some old jokes
And hopefully remember your laugh

But there's always a loneliness
That's riding on the breeze
It overpowers the scent
Of those sweet jasmine trees

I'll break out that old guitar
And play your favorite song
I hope that you still like it
I hope that you're still singing along

I'll bring you a bottle
Of homemade blackberry wine
I know you never drink it
But I bring it every time

We'll listen to a whippoorwill
That's calling from afar
Pick out the big dipper

And then the northern star

I'll have to be on my way
Before the sun shines through
Leaving nothing but my footprints
In the early morning dew

Late at night
Is when I need you the most
So I'll come walking in
Like a long grieving ghost

When I lay down on the dirt
We're going to talk for hours
And right before I leave
I'll water your flowers

To Face My Fading Light
Peter Rivers

This candle glows with special light
Even when the darkness comes,
it still remains so night light bright
In this window I dance and sway
behind a pane of glass that's gone away
A shattered past that haunts me still, alone I gasp
As if the wind grows super quick,
the more I twitch, the more I flick
Dancing desperation as hot as the fire of desire
Soaking me wet, sensually warm from molten wax,
that takes me back…
Time consumes all things
like this wick replaying my memory
They cut in and out as that very same flame
fades back into black
These eyes have gone and lost their light
Perhaps it is time that I said good night

Pearls
Ian Cave

The sandpiper knows
just where to find a morsel,
one passing worm, carried by the tide,
to find a new home.

The oyster hungrily awaits
its future companion;
the patient diver must hold their breath,
aware of the slow accretion of time.

The passing of moons
is necessary for the growth of wisdom.

The oyster must feel the intrusion,
secreting its shell,
layer upon layer
of mind polished lustre,
clouding the memory,
the mother of pearl,
a forgotten gift
waiting to be found.

The full moon returns every month,
as the pearl grows and the pain recedes,
tides of emotion flowing
from mother to child,
knowing that the time will come
when the oyster is opened,
to reveal the beauty within.

The neck of my love,
strung with pearls of wisdom,
reflecting in the moonlit sea.

Moonings
Scot A. Buffington

Stargazers of science
who navigate sex-tant
trace heavenly bodies
with fingertip's quill
seekers of knowledge,
empyrean intent
as Leo lays Virgo
at Regulus' will.

An indigo banyan,
three hues before midnight
of size sewn-for-two,
fitting Lady and Lord
well-figured satin
shines back to the moonlight
enraptured wrapped drapings,
two royal's accord.

Anticipants pine
for each twilighted rising
peek portals, astrologist's
sex-tile degrees
pulls gravitational,
full energizing
tide's ebbing and flowing
it gifts to the seas.

Waxing and waning,
each evening in motion
two transcendentalists,
one mystic's grasp
elysian powers
constellate devotion
form nebulae stellars,
from one conjugal gasp.

Shapeshifting moonings
reposit to crescent
still wound in cloak-robings,
jewelled with feldspars
curled, naked starings
of lovers coprescent
voyaging voyeurs,
awake with the stars.

My Pen Friend
Thomas B. Maxwell

Once I would compose letters
to a chosen few I knew,
but somehow it evaded me
what was going on with you

There was no pain I knew of
I heard not a whispered cry
for help, no disclosed origin
leading to where you would die

No burden did you speak of
that betrayed a gentle voice
No inclination did I have
that recognised your choice

To rid one's self from all the world
See no one, even I
made all the written words we shared
seem nothing but a lie

Then you were gone, still to this day,
the reasoning I missed
Like once you lived, then decided
to no longer exist

Spring Sun and Sadness
Susanne West

A bright spring sun
Bird chirping hours
Flowers seem glad to be back
Life-affirming green
adorning our town
Gardens breathing
beauty and goodness

and…..and…..
So many of the most
vulnerable in our world
afraid
hungry
hurting
lost
alone

Raindrops of grief
on this sunny April day

Wish I had a Home like You
Christine Gallant

Wish I had a home
  like you
But where I live
  it's something
  we can't do
I hope one day
I will not have
  to live in poverty.
And have a home
  like you

Mystical
R. David Fletcher

Stillness calls, her softness gleams,
A tribute to fate, to harbored dreams;
We are cast as one, as one He deems,
Lives converge, in textured seams.
Years ago, the heavens played,
Stars collided, and hearts were made;
Minds evolved, dues were paid,
Destiny laughed, and paths were laid.
Now the bond is formed, inexorable plight,
Your caress my eyes, I drink your light;
Our consummate hope, our lingering flight,
We fall and soar, in love's stark might.

Women
Tanya Raval

A mother, a wife, a sister, a daughter,
The unheard voices of many without laughter,
The daily grind of cooking and cleaning,
The looking after others before your own just giving,
Until the glass is half full or half empty,
They strive and work without compromise or pity,
Giving is in their true nature,
Through them the generations get their culture,
They sacrifice their own dreams
to support the dreams of others,
She lives and dies for you yet everyday
you are being beguiled,
You do not see her cry,
A strength in her persona so beautifully tamed,
She is here to stay no matter what life has gamed,
She is the embodiment of true spirit,
and yet she is not famed.

I Dreamed of Blue
Jennifer M. Nichols

Colours cocoon clouds,
to drip and dance
on fairy-floss fantasies,
to blend and bleed
luminous hues of blues
in delicate pas de deux
of plump periwinkle
and veiled lavender...

The Perfect Companion
Nadia Martelli

He thought they were
Vaudeville vermin
The way they behaved
Or did not
But he sought out their
Composite poison
To allay how he craved
His own hidden shot
He scoured sordid streets
All the blue-black night
Seeking the perfect
Companion
He devoured morbid feats
Like he knew of cracked light
Bleak his distorted opinion
One night he found it
All he yearned for
Had all his dreams
finally come true
Got to be right bound to it
Crawling to turn towards
Sadness falling through screams
Is that somebody you

Falling Home
Tracey Buster & Tim Queen

those beautiful leaves
silence they were
ignoring obstacles
falling softly with a plan

in their silence
crying not broken
softly with a plan
hearing their whispers

crying unbroken
awaiting the wind
loud whispers
refuse to understand

waiting for wind
birth of new life
refusing their demise
vibrant and calm

born of new light
awakened from sleep
vibrant unafraid
a place to rest

woke from slumber
shedding the wait
a resting place
longing to dance

tears of change
hues of wonder
longing to chance
seeking a home

Colors of Love
Patricia Woosley

White is the color of innocent love.
Soft like the feathers of a pure white dove.
Love of a father, who is true to the end.
Love through the years from a special friend.
Pink is love's color that I love the best.
Rosy pink flowers on her prom dress.
Beautiful music; lights glowing dim.
Blushing pink cheeks from her first kiss from him.
Red is love's color when its scorching hot.
Burning like embers, love sizzles and pops.
Blazing like the sun, high up above.
Yes, red is the radiant color of love.
Green is the color of love's jealous side.
Envy emotions and feeling denied.
Blue is love's color of feelings so sad.
Love's many colors, some good and some bad.
Colors of love through our lives how they glow.
More colors of love than the shining rainbow.
Colors so brilliant. Colors so true.
The many colors of love are waiting for you.

Seaside Senses
Micheal Jean Laswell

Swallow the squall the salted mist and hydration
Exhale the effluvium the bellowing of brine
Adjoin the creatures of the deep in isolation
Sense the pulsating of the waves overflowing
Identify the grains of silicon worlds below
Discern the calls and caws… the pitters and patters
Emotions rise and fall like rouge waves smashing

Late at Night on the River
Mike Rose

I feel at peace
When I'm deep in a dream
Like an old oak leaf
I'm being carried downstream

I never worry about the rapids
I know I'll make it through
And come out on the other side
Just a little black and blue

Guided by the stars
Pushed by the southern wind
I continue my journey
Up around another bend

There the water is calm
The world is perfectly still
And off in the distance
I hear my friend, the whippoorwill

All my memories are waiting
They're calling out my name
Lined up on the riverbank
Saying we're so glad you came

Those words touch my heart
It always makes me shiver
When I see them come to life
Late at night on the river

Mum
Beth Anne Nigro

She said, "I love you Beth,"
And squeezed my hand tightly;

I felt deep loss,
I never recall lightly.
"Why won't you eat?"
I asked her twice,
Never a response, just a glance
Still nice.
But her blue eyes are lost,
Her smirk, a silent pause.

Then I wonder "What are you thinking?"
For at this time, I have not an inkling.
(Now 87, she said)
"I feel my parents,
they're alive I know,"
I couldn't respond,
I did not know,
That love's so true,
That the distance is gone,
Time and space, thought far beyond.
That all that's left are
the letters from Scotland,
Now in mind, with reminders often,
Sent to and fro,
They're surreal to read,
And now there's none,
so please do take heed.
Scotland is here in blood,
and Celtic song,

But the dreamy ties to that place
have now come, and gone.

Grand Stage
Roland Wayne Bebler

On the grand stage
The play goes on

I've performed many parts
From lover to sinner to saint

I've been the joking clown
And old sage of wisdom

I've played these roles
And more
Sometimes in the same scene
Switching masks to hide me
Not revealing
Not letting the audience know
That behind the masks
Is a face
Cut with sadness
Vacant eyes and frowns
Cut with sorrows
And loss
With being many characters ?

I often wonder
Is the face sliced with tears
And sorrows
Just another mask?

I the actor
I the thespian
Question
Can I ever remember me?

Cosmic Conformity
Stephen James Smith

I have seen people fall
into a parade
of cosmic conformity
striving for more
hopeless dreams
of want want want,
their guts wrenching
with hungry ambition
feasting on the beast
of mouthwatering money
then choking on the vomit
of bills bills bills,
soon their desolation dreams
tear like open sores
bleeding obedience
into dreaded days
of work work work
passing slowly
like the storm clouds
they carry in their purses
holding them to ransom
until they're released
into the twilight
of their kidnapped life
where the sad sun
drops below the horizon
burning like a cremated coffin
their lives flashing before them
along a narrow road
of empty lives
strewn along
the wasted wayside
of cosmic conformity

Caliginous Saunter
Karin J. Hobson

Hush, my Darling let Crows speak
Black is the wing, Ebony it's wink;
Pinions flap, murder in sync,
Hush, my Darling let the birds sing
~
Haunt in tow, I push back the veil;
Onyx claw to fingernail, lip to tail;
Enigmatic stare, orb cast, beware
Kohl-black insinuates are paired!
~
Hush, my Darling, 'tis now complete;
Death by hand shall reign supreme;
Ivory-white bodice cinched and taut
Pale white bride is bleak and gaunt
~
Vouchered groom was Heaven sent
Tuxedo and bow alongside content;
Hush, my Darling, Gala's main event
went deep into the eye of Osiris
~
Moments clasping graveyard spade
Dabbling dots of crepuscular shade;
Caliginous cries permeate her mind
Eternal sleep saunters, lovers resign.

Soliloquizing
Kwaku Adjei-Fobi

A clot of thought eases its way, its sight glared by know-how of things hidden out of sight. "It is mo[u]rning" says he!
    'Mo[u]rning.'   Oftentimes it seems sunless in the mo[u]rning,   sunless, until you heave that frozen tear   out of the way!

Romanesque
Chuck Porretto

a little vault inside my heart
still holds a precious piece of art
beneath an arch of Romanesque
that sits above a school room desk
with yellow daisies in a vase
upon a doily made of lace
which recently would come to light
while kneeling down in prayer last night
-
It's just a little piece of art
beneath the arch within my heart
I painted back when I was young
and placed it where it's always hung
for I was shy and too afraid
to show the world the art I made
and so I hid it far away
inside the vault to always stay
-
but now I see this piece of art
with opened eyes and seasoned heart
and what I find to my surprise
is harboring of butterflies
that flutter through the vaulted space
above the daisies in their vase
to light upon a yellow bloom
as quivers echo through the room
-
today I reached inside my heart
and held the precious piece of art
to wipe the dust from off the frame
and light for it a little flame
that sits upon the school room desk
beneath the arches, Romanesque
which casts a glow upon the vase
and lights the portrait of your face

When it Started
Larry Bailie

Let me tell you what I'm thinking
Since the day I was born
I have been changing
In this thinking
I am sure I am not alone
Body and mind
Breathing and talking
Walking to running
Prideful and loving
You will get to the point
Where all the changes
Are so many like rain drops
Falling to earth
Seeds growing into harvested crops
Aging but setting up memories
Maybe others don't see it
Get it
Understand it
But it is clear to me
The final change comes
Like magic
I cease to be
I have changed
Miss me
Don't feel sorry
Not to worry
I have just changed
Like the rain drops
Falling from the sky
When we fall
We are never what we were
when it started

That's Just Dad
Tracy Taylor

my father's hugs
tight and all-encompassing
including a small amount of humming
as he embraces his children
we giggle at the humming
(and the tightness of the embrace)
yet would not want a hug without both
it is a sibling way of saying
"that's just dad"
every hug ends with
an extra tight pull
and, "I love you"
he still waits on the porch
when we leave
making sure he sees us
all the way home

My Heart
Catherine A. MacKenzie

My heart given to you that day
was a shaped stone found
upon the ground,
delicately, I brushed it off
and held it out to you—
a gem formed over time,
cold and hard as steel,
yet warmed with love and peace
from my hand to yours.

Maundy
Robert Atkins

At sixty-five I can't kneel down
For fear I won't get up again,
But Jesus, at age thirty-three,
Not only could but did.

I can't be arsed to wash the feet
Of people who won't do my will,
But Jesus, knowing who would lie
Knelt down and took the bowl.

When I can't face a troubled day
I pull the blankets up and hide,
But Jesus had the cross in view
And walked out all the same.

In what I call Gethsemane
I fall asleep to make it fade,
But Jesus fought away fatigue
And faced it up to death.

When someone sidles up to kiss
I kick and lash the traitor's name,
But Jesus, with his Judas there,
Was moved and stood amazed.

With all his knowledge, could he think
A friend would hand him to his foes,
A friend with feet still damp with tears
That, washing, Jesus shed.

An act of violence in the night
But Jesus reaches out to heal,
So maybe still, in age's spite,
I ought to try to kneel.

Too Much Grey
Valerie Dohren

There's far too much grey in the picture
The skies are meant to be blue
With greyness obscuring the background
Blandness depleting the hue

The world is designed to be coloured
Dipped in a palette more bold
With shimmering lights in the day-glow
Sunshine that's painted in gold

There's far too much brown in the image
Purple and red should be seen
The rainbow is painted in colours
And fields are depicted in green

The world is designed to be coloured
Yellow and bright is the day
Flowers in bloom are so lovely
Chasing the darkness away

There's far too much black in my heart now
A darkness I cannot conceal
I pray for a light to start shining
More colours to sweetly reveal

The world is designed to be coloured
The eyes should be vibrant and bright
Seeing all life in its glory
Bidding farewell to the night

Schumann Frequency
Ryan Morgan

Follow, follow,
Into the soft, pulsing places,
Where spirits of the stones
Sing to the turning land,
A song that rocks the rolling ring
Of this world's dancing swing,
Tethered from core to sun,
Connecting light and sound
As a harmonious one.
Lay your ear
And embrace
The breathing ground.
Slow your restlessness.
Away from the rush
You might hear
Earth's hot, hidden hum.
We all share vibration.
Resonate with this moment.

Find Home
Patrick Darnell

Sodden paths trampled
Into alleyways scurried
In empty backrooms scampered
I appear hurried
Were it a dissociative fugue
Point of shortfall to adjust
Where I've been I dispute
Caught like gentle dust
My claim is ever the same
I cannot remember my name.

Coming Light
Trude Foster

The world and all its many fingered thumbs
has me by the throat
tugging hard at the wire
gripping tight it cuts, sharp at the prospect of another hour
until I do not know if flesh is bone,
bone is flesh,
or something in-between,
all is pain, and pain is all
lightning in a head that is filled to the lips with rags and straw
raw alight and burning bright, although I wish it were not so
I want it dim to let me sleep,
let me hide in dull-thought darkness
calm beneath the leafy shedding midnight trees
with their echoed mindless hum
and owls, there are always owls
screeching brutes of talon tinted wings
that eat the other flying things that haunt my night
and I can only lay, and wait for coming light

Snowfall
Micheal Jean Laswell

Behold the world's death, at the end of all...
Frost shards float down like cherry petals,
As Infinite weightless moments of silence collect,
Rending the verth of life frozen still and stout,
Trees bathed in layered ice and dusted branches,
Permafrozen creatures huddled together hopeful,
A new terra one comprised of dread and discomfort,
The everlasting everything is rendered motionless,
Inhaling the icy winds the world breaths nevermore

What Would You Do?
Carol Lease

If I shared my secrets,
What would you do?
Treasure and keep them,
Or betray my trust too.

If I showed my spirit,
What would you do?
Help illuminate the light,
That wants to shine through.

If I surrendered my heart,
What would you do?
Passionately love it,
And forever be true.

If I offered up my body,
What would you do?
Cherish and caress me,
Like I need you to.

Icarus
Stephen W. Atkinson

I fell into a fever of dreams
Where nothing was as it seems
The world had changed, liberty frail
Captain Ahab vs the great white whale
I saw the moon turning red
The autumn leaves crisply dead
Underfoot and underhand
Fill the graves with shifting sands
When Heaven falls, Hell will rise
Through corporate suits and silken ties

Fix You
J. Henry DeKnight

We are tools
tools that rust
and squeak
    making noise
     like children's
     prized toys

    We sit silent
     on the shelf
     until needed
turn heads
as our wounds
bleeded

We preform
 like magic like
healing angels
    flapping wings
    to glow our halo
     to fix you

All the while
hoping,
praying for strength
    We are squeaky
     rusty
     tools

Caryatids
Linda Adelia Powers

In umbrages of pressures statues
Reserved reversing earth and heaven
Charged in stone unforgiven women
Breathing, searching faces braced in screens
Wishing to see across a freeing fleeing river
Blossoms floating upstream

They were the spirits of the trees dancing
Satyrs entwined them in pairing groves
Orchard pleasures oranges olives grapes
Pomegranates, treasured kitharas and flutes
Singing evanescing into starlight dreaming
A storm of fireflies visiting Olympus

Until by acts of self-protection condemned
Turned into more stable solutions
Solidifying statues fixed sculpted forms
Infinite influences of stony beauty
Stripped of limbs, roots, floor and rood
Glades and wooded streams denied

Courtyard and career of Artemis deserted
Temples of their lives now columned
Living dress of rude wraps made permanent
Spirits of spring forever petrified
Shadows of landscapes persist rising round
Warmth diffusing blazing sun encasing torsos

Angel Spirit of the stone, Holy Mother Chisel
If Titan left his canvas, walked among them
Could he resist his hand
Slope of thigh, chill buttock, soft dove
Drifting on dreams of the frozen goddess
Melting pacing steadfastly ahead and up

Beyond the temples swinging striding hips

Magnetically loosed from pole to lode
Trembling for the future north of brilliant stone
Their bodies effaced his burden embraced
Imagining they advance as he attracts directions
The world set on their crowns in lithic projections

Winged arms and haloed heads
Ruins humbly keeping us aloft
Standing hopping unsteadily
Forward from the edges of our ledges
As if memory will soon depart
As if we truly seek a pedestal
As if we could really fly
We gargoyles from Eden

Heartbreak
James Alexander Crown

Oh my soul and oh my mind!
I wish that fearsome wild beasts kind
Would feast upon my heart unkind;
Tear up the pulp, tear up the rind.
I gaze upon my mirror soul.
It mocks me saying 'two halves whole',
What crippling torment is this?
My heart's blood gouts, my brain a-fizz
With remonstrations and regret
And misery which pays a debt
Of hatred that my mind begets;
A madness casting heavy nets
Of loathing at my very core;
I quake, I could not love you more.

Time is Rhyme
Catherine A. MacKenzie

What is old age but a passing rhyme
Of minutes and hours merging in time,
Seconds depleted without a breath
Bring us all much closer to death.
We don't see time that seems to fly
By faster than the blink of an eye,
It's invisible, hidden within air,
Perhaps taken with the sun's glare.
We can search and search 'til day's end
For that elusiveness around the bend,
But we'll never find it nor capture it,
No matter how fast we race or flit.

Let's Dance to Peace
Tracy Murphy

Let your worries float away,
Like whispers on the breeze,
Let your tears evaporate,
Like the swelling of the seas,
Let your doubts be cast away,
Like the seasons of the year,
Let your resolve remain firm,
Against all it is you fear.
Let love dance into your heart,
Like a warm summer night,
Let hope sparkle and grow,
Like the stars shining bright,
Let happiness encircle you,
Like a hug from a teddy bear,
Let your mind know all's well,
And your soul be peaceful there.

If Poetry was a Crime
Jessica Ferreira Coury Magalhães

You're arrested for writing a poem!
Put your hands behind your back!
Blurted out the cranky sheriff
Nearly giving me a heart attack.

I did not write no poem!
I yelled to him in despair
I have an alibi, I told him
You can go ahead and check.

My pen ran out of ink
And I had not a piece of paper to spare
How could I have written a poem?
This arrestment is not fair!

Don't try to fool me, said the sheriff
I know you are mixed up with this poem affair
You had the opportunity and the motive
I know you're guilty, I declare!

I cried sheriff, you're mistaken!
I'm not involved in the business of rhyme
I don't even mix with those poetry folks
Babbling shabby verses all the time.

But the sheriff had hard evidence
A poem in my handwriting and style
With my fingerprints all over it
And he was taking me to trial.

I had witnesses accusing me
Of talking about the flowers and the sky
Of using fancy words to describe my feelings
That I was an "artsy" type of guy.

I took the stand and I confessed

It was pointless to deny
That I had indeed written the poem,
That I was guilty as was charged.

But I asked the jury for mercy
For it was a crime of passion I carried out
I was driven mad to the point of poetry
From the moment I saw your beautiful eyes.

Water, Hills, War
Patrick Darnell

Shall I commit to water
Enter the gorge and swim
Until I tire and can only float
Or commit to the promised land
When blizzard covers the hills
Walk to the tops until I stop
Or report to my outfit
March to the drum as trooper
To the front line
How can I go on believing
The greater of you is in me.
Welling bones bursted and thrown
Broken into your grotty fire pit
Of potash from matter, Aspen, and horsemint
And jawbone of an ass
Jutting out, a smoky mass
Turning watery eyes watery
Crackling, disturbing the harmony
In that wash of mountain yonder made
In end of hazy day in fixed array
Devoid color, denuded in end shade
Setting sun, fixed-time light dappled
Ordinarily beset in this battle.

Sands of Time
Gemma Tansey

Slipping through my fingers just like the sands of time.
I know that I would lose it as payment for a crime.

Reminisce the magic moment immortalized in signs.
Look for hidden meaning between the wavy lines.

Precious are the memories we forge along the way.
I'll immortalise the passion and ask if it will stay.

The last grain left in the timer of life!
Gritty and inscribed with the essence of strife.
Nothing can take this belief from me.
I close my eyes so I can see.

Please stay here and tend to my heart.
Freeze this moment, rewind to the start.
Don't tell me the magic has ever been lost,
Don't coat this grain in hard cold frost.

Keep it safe, and warm and keep it close.
Treasure the moments we valued the most.

The last grain of sand in the sands of time,
I'll do my best to make it mine.

And when I have it in my hand.
No longer is it grain or sand.

I'll give to you what I have to obtain.
One life, one soul in one small grain.

One small grain now two connected souls,
Combined together to fill the holes.

Time does not measure what we do,

So I'll take my time when I'm loving you.

Here is my grain it bears my pain,
But it's all for you and yours to gain.

So place the grain in your gentle grip
And please don't ever let it slip.

Feels
Simon Drake

A slippery slope, I'm sliding down
Embarrassingly dethroned, I've lost my crown
The humiliation is overbearing
It feels like even the blind are staring
Hearing laughter, cackling loud and clear
I'm dying inside, I want to disappear
Mouth dry, I'm speechless, nothing to say
Hoping survival instincts kick in, I have to escape
I'll run forever and never look back
Deep into the forest deep into the black
Debilitating voices hot on my tail
Their taxi, my mind that's what they hailed
There's no escape from my insecurities
My mental health's again got the better of me
Will it ever be kind, will it ever be fair
Will there ever be a time where I don't feel despair
Perhaps the day will break and the Sun will rise
The storm will subside they'll be a change of the tide
Until then, I think I'll feed on myself
I am the poison affecting my mental health

Span of Life
Gregory Richard Barden

a lifetime seen thru silence at your side
      from tiny lad to manchild in your shade
           one sole intent—to earn a nod of pride
   tho' I was never worth the effort made

in years past I had ears fast to the rail
      my tympans aching for the waking word
           that might let love or God above prevail
   but cold admonishments were all I heard

'hard work is how a father shows his love'
      how many times I'd heard that empty line
           but as you left the earth for heav'n above
   I learned the selfless depth of your design

what my self-pitied eyes could never see ...
      the mighty bridge that you had built for me.

The Meadow
George Valler

Sit now shall I with papered pen
The Heaven's blue cloud thoughts again
Write not of God, write not of waif
The centre line, my pen keep safe
Warm the sun climbs, climbs through the dawn
So rise today, tomorrow's morn
The meadow green, the yellow cup
Take now to flight, the bee will sup
Blue is the soft, the picture show
The flowered bloom, in nature's grow
Into the eye, the storm will sea
Foam and pounding angry be
Yet I may sit with papered pen
My dreams once more, I dream again

Opposites
Mike Rose

She loved the sun
I preferred the moon
She was as graceful as a swan
I was as crazy as a loon

She walked in the rain
I trekked through the snow
We danced in the wind
When it started to blow

She floated across the sky
I crawled on the ground
She could sing like a bird
While I barely made a sound

She was a beautiful flower
That was in full bloom
I existed in the dark
Like a wild mushroom

We were complete opposites
That were drawn together
Who somehow met in the middle
And became each other's forever

Kaleidoscopic Visions
Lorna McLaren

Kaleidoscopic visions fragmented,
crystal shards of disrepose,
coloured by the mental anguish
creating pictures uncomposed.
Changing moods of melancholy
strip bare the emanating gleam
turning then to shades of grey
till all there was goes unseen.
Kaleidoscopic visions falter,
blinking out one by one,
shadows recede into darkness
as to eternal sleep you succumb.
No more pain, no more sorrow
as you leave, your time now spent,
but your spirit free to discover
all that in life you only dreamt.

If Putin liked Children's Books
Hayley Sejberg

If Putin liked children's books
And invited me to tea
I would be concerned
About what was waiting there for me
Would there be a dungeon
For those wasting his time
Or a suitcase for your body
If you fail to fall in line
Would we play a game of Chess
The winner would take all
But then again
Nothing is fair
In Putin's game of war

Live Every Day
Richard Harries

You have been in the minds of mankind
Since the beginning of time
You have hovered and threatened and scared
You have been called many things
Have threatened the end and hell
You have been called the Angel of Death,
The Grim Reaper
The Ferryman over the River Styx
But all face you
And you will come
But we must not fear you
We must rejoice
Live and enjoy every day
We can make every effort to do this
We will not succeed every time
Some days there will be sadness and stress
But we must strive to make life count
and be full of pleasure
Then when you arrive you do not defeat us
As we take the next step into the unknown
That every soul has made since the beginning of time
Innocents, pure souls and the vile alike
Sleep can be wondrous and resting
And after the turmoil of life
Maybe we face rest
A sleep as in the fields of poppies of Oz
A deep velvety sleep as we carry on
Be gone death we will defeat your negativity

Yellow Bands
John C. Algar

As yellow bands
into orange meld,
the setting sun glows
o'er land and sea
and hills afar,
whilst blackbird sings and sings.

As evening's
light fades to dark,
blackbird's song it fadeth too,
until no sign of dusk remains,
when land and sky and sea
all blend into the one.
And all is completely silent now,
and all is silent now.

Speculation
Rachel Yarworth

In trying to write this little rhyme,
I found with great frustration
There were no subjects in my mind
That offered inspiration.
I could not write an epic verse—
My strength is not narration.
I realised, to be a poet
Could not be my vocation.
But after spending half an hour
Of solid application,
I suddenly found inside my head
A major transformation.
And now, although this verse of mine
Would not earn publication,
I've realised the only way
Is verbal lubrication.

Kensington Avenue
Charles P. Howes

This is no way to live,
rolling cigarettes with Prince Albert
and numb fingers.

Pulling fortunes from street puddles
Reflecting bending beams of yellow neon
and shadows of thirsty alley cats.

Watching stoned mimes bounce and tumble
like dice on concrete, others sit and warm
hands and hearts with friends of circumstance
around the rusty old burn barrels on street corners.

This is no way to live
Geared on Pookie fuel and counting
plastic bags that scurry down the street like
seagulls drunk on fermented Freedom Fries.

Moving through the world half dazed,
knowing but uncaring.
Sleeping in doorways with woollen collars
pulled close to waxen faces.

Eating the remnants of lunches left
by bankers and businessmen who point
snicker and sneer and call me
a rabbi of rags, while I think of myself
as a modern urban Thoreau.

This is no way to live,
rolling cigarettes with Prince Albert
and numb fingers.

Society
Bruce S. Hart

We are only one step further
From another person's breath…
While we amplify, yet multiply
Each step closer, to our death

Society, anxiety
Am I trapped within a web?
I'm swimming unconvincingly
And wish this tide would ebb

I march in time and sequence
Yet I'm walking out of step…
Do they notice out of pretence
That I'm feeling out of depth?

New moon, I swoon complacent
As I save another dime…
I wait forever patient
For my moment, with mankind

Unseen
Stephen W. Atkinson

Shall no one care?
Shall no one cry?
Shall no one come to say goodbye?
Not a single tear
Not a voice to hear
Not a stone to say, here I lie?
I am music without sound
I am nowhere to be found
I am a leaf that falls to die
I am the periphery of your eye.

Unsatisfied Desires
Anita Chechi

The desires of some beings
remain unsatisfied
To fulfil the unsatisfied desires,
the being takes birth again and again
And remains entangled in this bondage of karma
Among these, the most powerful
is the dissatisfaction of love
In search of which
the being wanders throughout his life
In the absence of love
He is overcome with sadness
Which is clearly visible on his face
He hides his sadness
In thousands of ways
But at the last moment
His patience breaks
And he expresses his anger.

Waxing Moon
Tom Cleary

The emissary of unbidden night
sits patient, waiting for his foe to set
in resignation, star that once burned bright
is now perforce to leave the scene and yet
retreats but just for now, regroups again.
The sickled eye of feline moon now fades
in slumber, pale, embarking it ascends
opposing sun at height of day through shades
opaque, half hidden, seeming old and frail.
Its subtle, sly and stalking stance now still
as quiet grows its radiance avails
those beams of light until it's had its fill.
As star presents its lifeblood for us all
sickly moon laps tides of beams until sun's fall.

Listen to a Stream
Chuck Porretto

Listen to a stream,
where the shiny pebbles gleam,
while the weaving water washes down a rill.

For the splash may spill a thought,
that will comfort when it's caught,
but you'll only catch it if you're standing still.

Listen to the birds,
warble wisdom without words,
let 'em lend their little lessons all along.

When you hum a happy hymn,
soon a soothing settles in,
for a solace sits inside a simple song.

Listen to the wind,
when a willing willow bends,
for its whisper is a winsome confidant.

There's an ease upon a breeze,
as it tumbles through the trees,
that will whisk away the worry and the want.

Let your nature give you peace,
and your running ragged cease,
for tranquility can help a heart to smile.

And the bird, the breeze, the brook,
have more answers than a book,
if we only stop to ponder them a while.

When you listen to the world,
every puzzle is unfurled,
and the present is a dandy day to start.

But you cannot use your ear,
for the only way to hear,
is to listen to their secrets with your heart.

I Will Find You
Sheila Grenon

I will find you
   As my words drift *awaaay*
Tears fall as I dread
   My words are important, I read.

~

You sleep as I stay awake
   Quiet slumber... Shhhh... Shhhh...
My protruding words ache
   As in this poem I cannot forsake.

~

Round one like a wrestler
   Not stopping just be-poppin'
My pens words fight to circumvent
   Needing them to ascend, not descend.

~

Quietness in these rooms
   My speedy pen just zooms
Just like the turbulent seas
   Some poems are a sad catastrophe.

~

I write them as I please
   Signifying a step to a higher decree
Few become my permanent
   Pleasurable adoptees.

Journey
Moazzem Hossain

We are moving
On this journey with no definite destination!
In this boundless, dimensionless voyage of life,
I only see tiny dots—
Dots rushing wildly in lines,
Forward and backward,
Up and down!

I see rivers, paddy fields!
Pale blue grass flowers blooming along the ridges!
I see the dim evening light,
the muddy chest of the Padma cradling hilsa,
The face of a river dolphin!
I see untimely floodwaters,
A baby waterhen nestled under its mother's wings!
Restless, darting, diving,
Seeking a snail's flesh!

Yet I see!
I see familiar faces, moments thick with events!
A bird once flew in—a heron,
Perched in the fields, waiting for fish!
That heron, that white heron,
Was shot dead by my uncle's double-barrelled gun!
That bloodshed still flows within me,
Like the sorrow of the krauncha bird!

Journey—ah, the endless path of journey!
From a single dot to a circle,
Drifting, burning, soaring,
From country to continent,
Crossing seas and oceans—
Where will it all end?
The manned vessel, the human tower?

A Shadowy Room
Kevin Francis

A shadowy room where flames jump through logs
Glowing crimson in the hearth
Tousled curls of grey roll across a balding pate
Tendrils of smoke rise from a bowl of sweet briar flake
A pungent aroma blends with the haze of heat
And forms a halo over the old wooden seat
It creaks in the shadows
Eerily defying me to be there
I will see this room so many times
Never again in life
Always in mind
A little corner where I can look at an ordinary world
A life I couldn't hold, when the page was turned
The child who slept on the broad leather couch
Slept through it all, within and without

Concrete Jungle
Donna Smith

Saturated towering skyscrapers loom heavy
Like spies watching from the sky.
Their pewter skin coalescing with the damp ashen fog
as they survey the city far below.
Row upon row of endless drab streets
form an interlocking impenetrable maze that no one can escape.
Like tripod gaited ants they robotically move, working in a
threaded network scuttling back and forth
shackled in their mundane captivity
And through thousands of soulless windows, they work
Caged and chained to this concrete jungle
But still clinging to the branches of its fabrication
Climbing, descending
Navigating every twist and turn
Knowing that someone, at any time may pounce
And take their pound of flesh.

Motherhood: Unfiltered
Jodeci Flores

Long hair, don't care—
or something like that.
My socks are mismatched,
and my nails? They've cracked.
There's frizz in my curls,
a far cry from a little girl's world.

Now I'm a mother, always sought after,
even hiding in the bathroom's no answer.
If it's not a baby, it's the cat,
or a knock at the door for some idle chat.
"Come back later, the time's not right,"
I mutter, just trying to keep things light.

Dinner's chaos, tater tots or gravy?
Chicken strips? Mozzarella sticks, maybe?
I plate the meal, they twist and squirm,
while the stove keeps a steady burn.
No ladles at the table, just petty squabbles,
dishes stacked so high, pray none wobbles.

The house is a canvas, its walls a gallery,
scribbled crayon art and handprint parodies.
"Kids, gather 'round, it's vitamin hour—
Flintstones lined up, fuel for our power!"

By eight o'clock, the house feels calm.
They're tucked in bed, no alarms.
And though my strength feels worn and thin,
I'll keep going—again and again.

She braved the jungle, ruled in the kitchen,
and loved in the sheets.
Wore her scars like hand-me-down heat.
Wrapped up the wreckage, made it her own.
Of all that I offered, let these three be known.

What is it like ?
Garrie Grant

It's like lighting a pyre of wooden ladders to climb up
waiting with a noose around my neck
to feel what it was like to be happy

It's always being right
except when it matters

It's never being right

It's like being at that place people talk about
"Beyond caring"
but being constantly winded by blows of empathy below the belt

It's knowing the stars look the same from the foot of the mountain
as they do from the top
but climbing up in bare feet just to throw myself off over and over again
because all deaths feel the same

It's being good at everything
except good enough

It's when logic is elongated into exponential tangents of infinite thoughts
then analysing diagnosing concluding
refuting and elongating into more tangents to over think about
It's thinking about how not to think

It's Russian roulette with five live rounds and one blank
but still being compelled to cheat to lose but always winning
except when I don't

You say that you would love to know what goes on in my head ?
I will let you know
when I know

Getting to the Other Side
Rachel Yarworth

The air has dropped a few degrees,
The darkening clouds draw near.
The boat begins to creak and buck,
Brave fishermen taste fear.
The rain falls from the death-black sky,
Assaults with cruel force.
The wind tears through the futile sails
And waves turn into walls.
The hostile sea now overwhelms,
The vessel starts to drown,
All cries for help lost in the fury
of the raging storm.
"Awake, O Lord, please save us now
Else we are going to die!
How can you sleep when such a storm
has come to take our lives?"
"Such little faith; why so afraid?
The other side's my will.
You need not fear when I'm on board,
So peace… be still!"
The wind and waves instantly tamed,
The little boat at rest.
The fishermen relieved that they
have made it through the test.
Dear Lord, when storms of life arise
to overwhelm with fear,
help us to keep our hearts at peace
knowing You are with us here.

A Dream in A Bookcase
Rafik Romdhani

Every day I hide a dream in my bookcase.
I read as much of it as I can.
I smell those old, yellow papers
and I place the spring rose there
in between the dormant pages.
Every day, I lean against the wall,
leaf through a dream with my eyes,
a dream coming out of darkness.
This blue book revealing a sailing hat
is mine, and this dried rose
inside of it is also mine.
The entire place teeming with metaphors,
the cigarette butts under the chair and table,
the ravenous barking of dogs are all mine.
My recognizant heart heavy with the snow
of the North is half mine.
I still remember you, tooth-gapped angel
You are here among my dreams.
You have become a unique cover art
for all the dead I haven't yet talked to.
You are a dream in a bookcase,
an irresistible bird in the sky of absence.

Sandstone Ghosts
Angela Brown

This poem is as close as we'll ever be.
The only safe space to touch you,
to gently run my fingers across your lips
and pull us into a kiss: a kiss like none ever written before us.
Fault lines of veins cut pulsing pathways down your forearms
as you pull me tightly into your stone body.

Pressed against your chest, in this poem: the only safe place I can press against you,
your kisses move from my lips in a trembling wet trail to my neck.
From coast to coast our daydream erodes.
I close my eyes once more.
Your hands, rigid and unyielding, grip me again.
Your mouth is on me again, as if to take over my entire territory
and carve into me your own immortal work of words—
making me beg for you to write for me!

Alone in your dark place,
the grey corners of your mind take their evil aim.
Close your eyes, dear.
Let us traverse this poem again.
These white hills of sandstone turn into the curves of my figure,
posing pale and soft beneath your caustic body of quartz and calcite—
mouth and hands in a frenzy to taste and feel every inch of me before this poem ends,
and we become ghosts, invisible poets,
a reflection alone,
between friends.

We are the only remnants left of an ancient time
when a strange mountain range crossed continents forever,
like twisted lovers rising from a dream forever.
Even the clouds seem to crave us,
making playful shapes above us as you push inside of me,
the wind beating us like a battle drum,
my fingers dig into you, as we come
to the end of this page.

Rivers of wanting have carved out a jagged shoreline through my heart,
and I bleed into dust for you.
This is the torturous movement of all things across time: love slips through our fingers like grains of sand, lands separated by an ocean of ache, waiting for the end of earth
to break.

The Dawn River
Moazzem Hossain

I have hidden away
A white, fragrant handkerchief in my bedroom!
Every night, I secretly touch it—
As if jasmine blooms at dawn,
As if a white dove takes flight!

Jasmine, oh jasmine,
Bloom within my soul,
Pour your scented rhythm
Into the sun-dappled woods!

I immerse myself in deep meditation!
For a fleeting moment,
I travel across distant shadowed paths,
Seeking Him, seeking my own self!

Then, riding on a horse of light,
I call out—
Where are you, where are you,
My hidden treasure, my beloved Saki!

I have secretly kept
A white, fragrant handkerchief in my bedroom!
Every night, before I sleep,
I inhale the scent of jasmine!

Jasmine, oh Jasmine,
Bloom within my soul,
The dawn river, in its silent dive,
Has touched the depths of solitude!

Pink Moon
Tracey Buster & Tim Queen

I'm reaching back
along winding roads
to find what can
never be remembered

along a mountain road
a man is lying still
I can hardly remember
in the glare of the headlights

a man lays dying
a woman is waiting
one broken headlight
shivers reaching home

a pink moon crying
she's picking up the phone
a man's spirit rises
children still are playing

she falls to the floor
time is silent listening
shiver in the moonlight
church bells are ringing

along a mountain road
a man is still remembered
a woman is still waiting
a pink moon is rising

an old broken headlight

Alcatraz
Simon Drake

How do I unplug from you
Frayed wires still run through my heart
Entangled within my love and feelings
Sparking intermittently
I'm still connected by the torture I endured
At your soft and beautiful hands
You totally devoid of empathy
Your wickedly callous nature
Put me in an everlasting trance
Trapped by your radiant hypnotic beauty
Your true nature hidden
Deep, under hell itself
I died a thousand times a day
In your presence, abuse the gift
You wrapped with a bow over a ticking time bomb
Served with sweet kisses and hours of passion
You destroyed me over and over
After every rebirth I searched for you
Every time I rose from the ashes
My heart sought you out
There is no rationality to be found
Common sense brutally discarded
Eventually, overtime, my sane mind snapped
I plotted and planned becoming as calculated as you
I kidnapped my own heart
Forced to escape from your Alcatraz
It's been months which have felt like decades
Multiplied by a million lifetimes
Yet my heart still pines for you
Like a loyal and loving dog
Whimpering for its lost master

Love Beats
Sharon Toner

Love beats …

With the weight of your fears
Your angst and need
The panicked turmoil
That lies in wait
Beneath the surface
In your heart's shadows
Between all of that
And love's arrows

Love beats …
Love beats …

In stifled breaths
Tripping over stumbled words
That are sometimes
All too hard to hear
But need to be said
Nevertheless
For honesty needs to be
Expressed genuinely

Love beats …
Love beats …

In hesitant pauses
In touching little moments
Heartfelt caresses
That entwine from the soul
Wrapping around
Until you feel whole
In your entire being
Given unconditionally
Love beats …

Live Alone
Rafik Romdhani

Live alone!
and choose for yourself a door
that opens onto the embers of the desert.
Don't say after the death of the trees
you still have a homeland,
and scoop up the water that quenches
your thirst with your own hand.
Live alone
like the sound of the wind, like a daisy
whose feet are still steeped in the ashes,
whose green leaves are certain wings
despite the trampling of hooves.
Don't say that after the sky there is a mirror
to the blood of birds
or half a dream for them under your pillow.
Live alone
like an introspective window in a wall
And say nothing to your solitude.

Gloom Quickens
Martha M. Miller

Heavy slate clouds hovering,
tinged by fire, covering
the near horizon.
Hazy smoke fingers rise on
air currents before dawn
tickling waning stars
through the portal left ajar
by night's cagey escape
from the dark cloudscape.
April showers set the stage
for Resurrection Day
and the Passion play,
gloom quickens new life's array.

Dancing into the Uncertainty
Iain Strachan

Whirling circle of prayer
Keeping the wheel whirling
Circle of swirling prayer
Keeping it turning till the end ...

Drawing its arc on the floor
Writing unknown words in the dust
Eternal praying—eternal circle
Gyroscoping in prayer
Hanging steady
In angular momentum.

Dance the prayer
Pray the dance
Dancing into the uncertainty,
Dancing through tears
Of bright sadness to joy.

Keeping the Cyr wheel circling
Wrapped in this sacramental cycle
Of systole and diastole,
Beat after beat in sinus rhythm repeat.

Dancing on the ridge of stability
Praying in the strange tongue
Of looping movement;
Cursive gestures into unknowing
Leaping through its gyrations
Acting on what is at hand.

Standing aside and meditating on its moment
As it turns and swirls to itself
Then hurling your own momentum into it
Becoming an X of limbs,
Of feet and hands attached,
Encircled by its rippling rim,

And whirling with it
Circling the prayer
Winging to its rhythm.

Living with the uncertainty
Unknown when it will end
Unknown when this earthly wheel stills
Still dancing to the rhythm
Of inspiration and expiration
And greet that final dying
Of mortal light,
Breathing, into the uncertainty,
Into the unknown Light beyond.

Carcassonne
Kate Cameron

Tiers of sunlight slanted on the stone
noble pillars cast blue shade
as narrow poplars by the Seine

ancient medieval marketplace
heated by a southern sun
flowers blazed that day in Carcassonne

drinking Cafe, only I au lait
the picture catches as it's laid away
A murmur of mixed voices, memory
sharp and sunlit, then alive

now wreathed in vine leaves
placed to sleep,
where the river Garonne lies
dark and deep.

Village of the Lost
Lorna McLaren

Empty streets of ancient echoes,
limpid pools of yesterdays,
silent windows ever staring
at what was whole now in decay.

The ghostly sound of church bells peal,
a distorted call to come to prayer,
once so melodious and sweet
now melancholy in their despair.

Swallowed by the tides of time
a village lost to watery grave
and for those who lived within,
gone forever, none left to save.

The flood from out of nowhere came,
it happened oh so suddenly,
no warning as to what became their fate,
they had no time to think or flee.

Their spirits wander, left in turmoil,
trapped, there's no way they can leave
while in the empty streets of echoes
they speak only of their disbelief.

To see the lake you'd never know
the secret held within its depths
and all the souls who lost their lives
will never be empowered to rest.

Long forgotten no-one remembers
but this lake gives off an eerie feel
for when passing by you'll hear their whispers
and now and then the ghostly church bells peal.

Connecting Dots
Natasha Browne

Where would we be,
Without our poetry?,
Without our need to write?
Without our light?
What would I do in the night?

Sleep?

Thats funny.
You see,
Poetry
Keeps me awake,
It's like my mind shakes.

Shakes out words that rhyme,
As I climb,
Into bed,
Words float around my head.

As I tuck my head into the pillow,
I bellow,
Out words,
That go into a poem,
Even when I'm alone.

In my zone,
Under the duvet blanket,
I thank it,
My next write,
So, I get up,
Turn on my light.

Write some more,
Explore,
My three in the morning thoughts,
I connect the dots...

A Mile in Your Shoes
Larry Bracey

I think I get it now,
After walking a mile in your shoes,
Fighting every step of the way,
To survive a life you didn't choose,
Penniless and tired,
Driven but alone,
Never feeding into the belief,
Your path was written in stone,
Making hard decisions,
Leaving people in the rear view,
Realizing those left behind,
Weren't meant to come with you,
Because every step you took
There was something new to learn,
Every corner has a twist,
And that twist has a turn,
You've encountered forks in the road,
Which you took the time to read,
Taking one way leads to failure,
The other means you'll succeed,
My feet still ache,
From walking a mile in your shoes,
I pray you reach your destination,
Because I know you've paid your dues.

Chainsaws
Neil Mason

Chainsaw batons conduct old fashion music
Dead musicians are decomposing
Trees chopped to pieces
by chainsaws' deadly tunes
Right down to the Bach

Another Soul's Shoes
Graeme Stokes

If you haven't walked another's unique passage,
faced their pitfalls, survived their plights
Witnessed their bleeding feet get savaged,
'cause they couldn't locate bright light

If you haven't been part of their complex picture,
the vital detail within their whole
An absent ingredient from their mixture,
a sustaining flame to warm their cold

The daunting heights that they were forced to scale,
the falls from grace that plagued their heads
Smelt the pungent odour of their worlds gone stale,
the velvet coffins that be their beds

Felt the deadly heat of their stifling times,
with no shelter from the glare
Been lost in the maze of their transient minds,
no firm base to placate despair

If you haven't ingested another soul's pill,
digested the meals that they had to swallow
Recognised in their eyes a strength of will,
to fill the void when their space is hollow

If you've never had to sweat in another soul's skin,
felt the weight of their arduous toil
Not endured the burden of their guilt ridden sins,
the torments that will forever soil

If you don't know how deep be their lifetime's bruise,
how far they be lost at sea
If you've never stepped into another soul's shoes,
then choose to be judgement free

The Abolition of Warmth
Brandon Adam Haven

Wearing tired fleeces of paths long flown,
Denied again the crimson sky,
Thundering blood in the rains below,
Where sons and brothers go to die.
Flayed in a lost calling, they splatter 'neath
The hidden pendulum of love's undergrowth,
Thrusting the blade in archaic swift—
Where life's grasp orders death.

Faithful men and women beheaded,
This jaded form worn and weathered,
Its vibrancy laden in crowned canorous,
With sunken Horus in time's lost essence.
Wailing, sickened walls, wallowing gait,
Where rotten dawns the smile of cold,
Glittering with each rain, a mummified scold

Here I lay in the abolition of warmth.
Shaking, ready for my next withdrawal,
Scarfed words on dim balconies breathe,
Where oceans shed their arid wreath,
Castling wealth in ripples forgotten.
Embodied through the hallway screams,
Shelters cradle my failing dreams,
Torrid whispers by midnight's creek—
Where I learned of intoxication and woe.

People who forsake this pernicious place
Oftentimes do die alone;
I've never known nor felt at home,
My demented delve into existential dread
Leads me astray from a healing head.

Beat and Breath
David Catterton Grantz

The brain, poised upon its stanchion,
Considered all possibilities.
It had not known such grief.
This was something new.

It was fond of gazing outward
At the universe of stars, as
Now, in sorrow's abyss, it probed
The white-hot cores of quasars.

How austere, this diversion from
The sear of human angst.
Next, it hovered above daisies in the field
Some drooping, some basking in sunshine,
Others mere broken casualties merging
   with the thatch.

Its ego sought some dispensation,
Escape from nature's glorious indifference.
But only sadness presided, as it braced
Eyebrows before the pitiless torrent.

A hand and arm thrust inward.
The brain swivelled and formed its face.
As she drew him close; their hearts, their breaths
Enraptured, he felt the pulse of cosmos quicken.

Then, quite suddenly, he knew!

The Roots of the Soul
Anemone Rosendal

I can feel your roots in the ground I walk on
I can feel you in the wind,
in the branches and leaves of the trees
and your scent in every flower I see
We belong together
You live in me until the day
I stop breathing.

Haunted Verses
Jou Wilder

You're here in my verses—
almost alive
breathing into my sweaty palms
as I trace trembling words on bound paper.

The hungry hands of my thoughts
still drift through your hair—
the strands are strewn here—
everywhere—
thick, curly black hair.

Your smile, your voice, your laughter—
they haunt these pages.
I find you in every line
even the alphabet chases you today.

You were never in my verses
yet you haunt these lines—almost alive—
nearly whole, as you always were
struggling to return to life.

The Bewitching Hour
Jamie Willis

The heavens slipped into something more comfortable
Donning delphinium blue silk and bijou birthstones
Shimmying past Orion's belt
with a coyly crooking fingered invite
Ursa Major dips with urgency
Collecting asterisms to sustain the night

The spread above and waters below pantomime
their longings through the wind's propulsive gasping blow
Each lapping wave, each moonshaft pierce
Each set to the orchestral swell of fiercest howling wolves
and shrieks of owls ... intensity that's offset
by the softness of a firefly tease
and lakeshore late night summertime breeze...

I am awash in the glow
Suspended above, descending below
I'm a horizon splay, ambrosial in the bed
of the Kármán line and drenched in Milky Way.

My eyelids flutter, while telescopic tantra
keeps my third eye pinned awake...
My body flushed aurora pink
in places soft, in places deep
I sink into the rippled edge of universal conscious brink
At half-past nova, a cock crow cuts
the pressure of an atmospheric tangle
Lazuli satin slips away and tides retreat to proper place
And all that's left of their last embrace
Is my rosy pink and starry eyes
And ache to voyeur night time skies
Again.

The Flower
Mark Heathcote

Where does a flower go, Father?
When it has flowered,
Inwards or outwards?

Child—it doesn't matter
All that matters is,
That it has flowered
And took root within your soul.

Father, shall it die?
When the ice covers it,
Will it perish from the cold?

Child—it doesn't matter
All that matters is,
That its roots have entwined
Your heart and you can never die.

Father, am I a flower too?

Yes, my son, in the Garden of Eden

Father—where is this Garden?

Focus, child; look around you.
Inwards or outwards

Does not this love unbridle you?
Are you not a flower too?

The Sea of Dreams
Colin Hunt

I woke in the morning, to watch the sun rise.
I looked around, and knew nothing had survived.
As far as I could see, all was laid to waste.
I opened my mind and felt the hate,
From the earth towards the human race.

The enormity of it all sunk in, and I began to cry.
It was all true, the human race was doomed.
The earth so happy that we are history.
God's other creatures singing new songs.
Full of happiness because we are gone.

I awoke again, thinking it was all a dream?
Still full of sadness for all that I had seen.
Then a new sun rises across the land.
Bringing a rush of fresh air for me to breathe.
Is now the time to hope and believe.
My mind reaches out and I feel no response.

The earth so quiet, was something wrong.
Totally amused, I smiled once more.
I believed then, that we had a second chance.
Some miracle supplied by the almighty.
The sun rose once more across the land.

Making me believe once again.
Earth giving us one last chance.
To repair the damage we have done.
To live once more in harmony.
Then I see a human face, so full of hope.

My reflection upon the Sea of Dreams.

Dawn of Hope
Scott Barnett

There is a certain calm just before dawn...
Seems so long since I stopped to see one.
The still of the night, penetrated
with faint beams of light.
But as I look to the sky,
there's a watering in my eye.
I can't help but wonder why?
We sit back just watch it die.

Over the horizon the light peaks,
I close my eyes, then my mind speaks.
What are we doing to our home?
The place where giants, and tyrants use to roam.
We need to stop before it's too late.
How much more can Mother Earth take?
Why do we do the things we do?
Burn through resources like we have no clue.
What happens when they're all gone?
You can't act surprised, we knew all along.

And as the sun rises into the sky,
The light pierces my watering eye.
I hope that one day we learn to see,
That we can't survive without the tree,
Or the ant, the bear, the lion, or the bee.
And with this new dawn....
I hope our earth doesn't have to continue to bleed,
Because of our monetary greed.

Contrast
Richard Harries

Two motorways meet
Tarmac, white lines
Cats eyes, iron crash barriers
Bleak
A sweeping bend
A glimpse
Of water
A deep river
A flash of white
Majestic, ancient, historic swans
Brilliant against the dark of the water
The lush greenery of the bank
And then an arid wasteland
Flat leading to
Vast overwhelmingly large
Power station chimneys
Huge steel pylons
A contrast
So great
Nature and what humankind has
Done to it

Chaotic World
Ceba Sanelisiwe

Don't drown in the chaotic world,
Mankind is demolished by the noises,
Noises of pain, angst and frustrations.

Mercy now is a daydream
Of the kind men.
The world is a mess that no one can wrap up.

Mother Earth is full of tears,

Shuttered by men's envious actions.

It's no longer a normal day without a fight,
Nor a peaceful night without tears.

Kindness is crying and calling out in a tomb,
But no one can hear.
No one can save her,
Because she's deep inside the Earth's womb.

The world is now a wild,
Filled with wild animals dressed as humans.

Defying the Odds
Donna Smith

You're playing with fire
Skating on thin ice
Out on a limb
Rolling the dice
Taking the plunge
Walk the tightrope
Treading dangerous steps
Down a slippery slope
Taking a risk
You're asking for it
Going to get burnt
Going to get bit
Sticking your neck out
You hang by a thread
Never listen or hear
To a word that's been said

Defying the odds
All left now to chance
But you only live once
Time for one final dance

A Poem without Words
Jessica Ferreira Coury Magalhães

I want to write a poem without words
With just a cloud instead of a verse
I want the letters and the rhymes
Replaced by the brightness of the sky.

A poem without words
A white room filled by light and sounds
No paper, no ink, just sensations all around
And we'll melt into the singing of the birds.

Words are like death, written on a tomb
I want this poem to be alive and breathing
Growing like a child in the womb
Thunderous like a heart that's beating.

I want to write a poem without words
To be felt, not read, by all creatures
Like the placid water the pebble disturbs
A never ending poem beyond all speeches.

Midwinter Lives
Sean Timms

Evermore the silver birch
slim limbs covering a sylph-like form
flaking paper trunks glowing softly like ghosts within a fog
Sinewy shoulders and silver sheen
Silver shadows on silver streets
As naked fractals dance beneath dark, oppressive skies.
Waif-like leaves prance in the wintry breeze,
flirting and fluttering in a skirt of silk snowflakes
Ever more the silver birch

The Art of Conditioning
Taylor Juliet Ashton

people who write words
paint pictures
and make art
are valuable

but are conditioned
sadly
to get lost
in the numbers

it is human nature
to seek validation
but
at what cost?

our perspectives
are warped
by social media
looking for quantity over quality

we seek five thousand
instead of five
when five people
is still a crowd

five people
liking your art
is still five people
noticing you

and you should be proud
no matter who
or how many
people see you

for who you are
and for what you do.

Mature Outrage
Martha M. Miller

Call me old will you?
Hold my beer and watch this!
Yes, my knees may creek
and I may hiss,
but I can still climb a ladder, fool.

I still have the same creative heart
that graffitied walls and rail cars,
when the police wailed on scene
I was far
gone, with a bird's eye view
of the art.
Call me out of touch?
Give me that ladder and hear me
for I will use it as a podium
to speak
of history, what I have lived,
seen, so much.
I am unafraid and still have a voice
I will speak out against injustice,
I will speak my truth,
preach the need for kindness,
compassion,
and scream that we all
have a choice.
You are not alone in this world.
You may have youth, but
not acuity.
Your eyes may not be cloudy
but you still do not see far forward.
Call me old and dissociate
but read my graffiti
and auscultate.

Meetings
Shweta Bhide

Meeting a person at a meeting,
I want to call it fate
Meeting the same person by fate,
I want to call it a coincidence
Creating that coincidence to meet the person,
I want to call it an infatuation
Thinking about the person just after the meeting,
I want to call it an attraction
Losing the sense of time while meeting the person,
Well, all of us want to call it love
Living with the same person throughout the years,
We know! It's just an effect of all such meetings.

Metamorphic
Dale Parsons

Mineral rocks, in their radiance softly crackle
Here in the bubble beyond the night
Here, all is in colour
No heavy heart in this light
Let the door close behind, walk into bright new dawns
The ribbons of colour will cajole
all guests into each idyllic morn
Breath deep the vibrations,
and crackle with radiance as the rocks do
…all become mineral here
Here, in the never-ending horizon of purest joy,
exquisite in its wilderness
Move forward with no fear
The door is but a speck now, a pin prick return to the dark
In the brightness, all exits fade, another radiant rock is made
Flesh and bone into mineral stone
From the colours the bubble offers no shade

triolet o' chocolates
Matt Elmore

take me away, oh delicious bliss!
assorted morsels of addictive good taste!
I long for more of your sensuous kiss!
take me away, oh delicious bliss!
though my conscience disagree, I cannot miss
this dark rich bittersweet tryst in haste!
take me away, oh delicious bliss!
assorted morsels of addictive good taste!

Taraxacum
Jamie Willis

We are all here lightly
Tiny-born and frail
We float through hours like dandelions
Sometimes sticking to the lips
That blew a kiss of our potential
To the sanguine wind that's powdered with
The feather-things and samaras

I'll run my thumb across your lips
That exhaled hope to happenstance
I'll kiss away the cypselae
Nictate my lashes into yours
Where all the lightness of our innocence
Finds my sight to see us
Your arms to hold us
Our words to love us
In the other's remex flight across Oceanus
Just to give our light a sacred chance
To be witnessed for remembrance.

The Pain of the Oyster's Pearl
Sharon Toner

Life is full or irritations
But we can change these
The way we view them
The way we react
Is all up to us
The Pearl is made
From the oyster's irritation
Forming layer upon layer
It protects itself
But also healing the wound
In the process
Producing something beautiful
Transforming what was once
The pain of the oyster's pearl
An irritation or wound
Into a precious beauty.

Fiesta of Sunset
Sean Timms

Today whispered its farewell
the sun a molten orb of gold
the rainbow sky everclear
My soul clenched tightly in this sadness of mine
light shining dim upon my window pain
tears falling like grey rain from my mind's eyes
time always short when listed by sunset
As stress lives within its measurement distance
Sunsets ephemeral flames burn
in the once deep rich blue dye of my summer sky
The sunset and the evening star
 I wish I knew someone who could translate my whispers

Nothing
Linda Falter

Nothing is an empty space, a lost love
An expressionless face
Pain is hurting, and never seems fair
Endless sorrow, sadness, and tears
Afraid of all our greatest fears
A silent cry, a story without an end
You without a friend, me without you
Nothing is felt or heard when no one's there
To speak a word, nothing is an empty space
A lost love, and an expressionless face
Nothing is an empty space...nothing...

Angel of Death
Brandon Adam Haven

Angel of Death, release me
Burrowing in empty reminiscences,
Where I was never guided.

Let me graze your silken black wing,
To relinquish the lonesome sting.
For I have never mattered…

Please take heed to my silent lyres,
Quivering in dawn's grey bruise,
Floating amiss empty gales.

Oh, Angel of Death, unbind me!
The oblique of time is torn again,
As is my soul stirring within.

My Son of Sunshine
Eric Aguilar

Your soul shines bright.
To my beloved son of mine,
through the entirety of your life,
you are the rays of the sunshine.

Ever since you were just a baby,
you have been connected to the sun.
For, the light that's shining in you,
makes you equal to its sum.

God gifted you with high resolve
and a chiselled, whittled hardness.
You are a gift to this world and
your heart's a lighthouse in the darkness.

Your soul shines bright.
To my beloved son of mine,
through the entirety of your life,
you are the rays of the sunshine.

Your fight for life emits from you,
your light a shimmering blaze.
You are the glow of daylight
and illuminating is your space.

Your face glistens,
so much that your eyes smile.
You are the place where dusk and dawn
make peace and reconcile.

Your soul shines bright.
To my beloved son of mine,
through the entirety of your life,
you are the rays of the sunshine.

When the Storm was Over
Kate Cameron

I rolled under your wave
with pebbles and seaglass
with mermaids' purses
I drifted out on dark waters
the shore only a pale line under the moon
and when the storm was over
there was some kind of peace
a sprinkle of stars
sometimes I glowed with phosphorescence
sometimes I could not see my toes
lately the Canada geese cry, I hear the thwack
of wings
but they are invisible
I lived at all the pulses of the compass
but none was true north, home.

The Church
George Valler

How dark surrounds the history
Laid deep within these walls
so join the chorus, voices sing
Purple sits above the halls
The quiet lays its gentle hand
Before the wake of day
Let me then lord above the land
Come the morn, the dawn affray
If coloured dreams so paint of me
Away, sweep the web of years
The chorus sing in joyful sound
Let soft gently rain the tears

Poetry is Me
Graeme Stokes

I will never be a close friend of a Mercedes Benz,
I've just never possessed the drive
Besides I was the lone wolf that bucked the trend,
my mind steered to alternative climes
I never hatched ambitious plots for luxury yachts,
to bathe in the seas of lurid wealth
Follow the sheep's expectations
while my inner self rots
and atrophies on the shelf
I've never sprinted headlong after fame and fortune,
I'm oblivious to what sits in the bank
I just thank God I've been dealt large rich portions
from my imagining's bottomless tank
My passion is lustily stirred by the written word,
the fuse to ignite my mission
Trailblazing my concepts to spiritual worlds,
the shaman to facilitate visions
Ideas twitch alive in every fibre,
as my head puts on lavish spreads
of golden nuggets and off the cuff diamonds,
sparkling infinite paths and threads
It's my fur coat against the winter cold,
my relieving cool summer breeze
It's my troll that crosses bridges bold,
resolute roots that grow my tree
It's the blood that circulates my whole,
my beating heart's jump leads
every breath I breathe,
lodged in my soul,
yes poetry is me!

The River
J. P. Hayter

To the river
I have been so many times,
It's beginnings secluded in a valley,
Where once we feasted like royalty above its banks,
in shadow, and in golden light,
To the river that I have been so many times,
To watch the daylight turn into night,
Though on this day I maybe far away ,
And lost in another's plight..
(You may be somewhere else instead),
Still the seasons come and go,
On this the river, that never stops her flow,
I may yet return in sleeveless summer shirt,
Or in winter's coat...
To watch the dappled sunbeams
on that spot where we first embraced,
Now a melancholy sight,
Yet so still the sun looks on,
Unblinking,
Maybe you think I am with another now?
But, no, in my mind I am still with you,
'Tis a moment of great beauty too,
So obscured, hidden so thickly in the folds of time,
Almost too sickly for my mind to find!
Yet I have found us!
There, standing on the road to Monmouth,
Somewhere in the not too distant past,
You turned to go,
I kissed you..
I know now, but could not know it then,
I was destined to follow that winding waterway,
Snaking through the deepest wooded valleys,
And I was lost..
But now, oh that I could take myself
away from here, never to return,
Back to the River wise,

Where she lies, wide open, and whispering to the sky!
Right here, on this spot, where she met the old ruined abbeys gaze!
It held her strong, meandering slow, trapped in the past,
Till the present called her and she mixed in her unbound love;
And it was there that you held it in your trembling hands;
A flower!
A sacrament to our holy hour!
And so this was how the river,
The River
Found herself all at sea!

Are you Hiding like Me?
Angela Brown

What is burned in me cannot be reborn.
Afterbirth is just before death, and I've heard
damnation is a priceless form of forever.

I've been marked—Diablo darling,
howling halo since conception.
Are you hiding like me, covered in leaves
biding time before the Rhyme Master riddles us blind?
I want to confess this to you: I am terrified
He will snap my pen at the tip, drowning my gift
with every black ink drip,
drip,
drip…reducing me to a memory,
to nothing.

This page is all I have, the only place
I feel safe to pour out my desperate longing for dark things,
pin pricks and bloodletting, a holy abomination,
fourth horseman's chorus of consonants and vowels…

Will you cradle my little poems to your chest
and give them purpose?
Will you take me tonight,
that I don't die in shame?

September
Roland Wayne Bebler

It bloomed with so much hope
In the spring
Like early flowers
Giving birth to dreams
And grew intensely passionately
Though the summer months
Now brutal bitter assassinating
Late autumn winds
Whip heart bare trees
That cried their last tears
In October
Over the September death of
Our summer love

Where You End and I Begin
Matthew Burgio

It's us that makes the world spin,
Entangled in our lovers' state,
And where you end and I begin
Is bound by love in line with fate.

We lay there in a figure eight,
Wrapped up as one as close we lay.
We'll make forever of this day
As both our hearts with love we sate.

It's bound by love in line with fate,
This, where you end and I begin.
Entangled in our lovers' state,
It's us that makes the world spin.

Burning Absence
Stephen James Smith

It was that time of year again,
hoping for a still dry darkness
absent of burning November rain.
We waited as children,
mouths wide open,
drawing in cool air
and warm expectation.
You opened the fireworks box,
pulled out a rocket and lit it,
it sparked, fizzed, roared alive:
we were born into this great expanse
of time and energy and life
flying like baby birds from your hands
circling streams of stunned stars;
you warmed us with smiles,
lit up blazing candles in our eyes,
zoomed love into November's icy heart,
boomed life into our worlds.

Within seconds, it was over.
Gone into the puff of a vast vacuum,
extinguished of sounds, light, life.

Gone. Like you.

And now, all we hear
are the deafening echoes
of your burning absence
scorching our hearts
like a rocket
with the saddest sweetest pain
over and over and over again.

Purplicity
Sarah Sansbury

Vibrant, exultant, royal
making no apologies for its entrance
purples may exaggerate and swagger
but they hold all boasting rights.
Violet, boysenberry, lavender,
grape, periwinkle, iris,
their very names a powder compact
Time to break them out
no need for old age's excuse
to pop and flounce through the world
in heather, mulberry, magenta
mauve, sangria, aubergine
lilac, plum, orchid
nature's finest
rejoicing in juiciness
all parade their glory
And so shall we
Purplicity!

Eclipse
Bruce S. Hart

So bright the day before me
How quickly things can change…
Perhaps another story
And a chance to rearrange

I swear I thought I saw you
From the corner of my eye…
Your shadow cast, upon my past
At a time, I can't deny

In solitude, ineptitude
I have no answers left…
Your attitude, in amplitude
Allows your case to rest

Then suddenly, incredibly
The sun comes back so bright…
But as it were, we can't concur
And the day turns back, to night

Confession
Kendra Bower

this is not a poem
this is a confession
for every time I missed the mark
for every time I broke a heart
or had mine broken by a world of the unknown
and unrequited
I have drowned myself with indecisions
steeped time in bitterness and regret
I confess, I have not learned my lesson yet
truth and dreams are heavy things
each one has its cost
it takes courage to bridge the gap
I lost myself to chaos, gave up control
and know I will never live to know
I confess that I will never know
the beauty of the child that I let go
I confess to watching every season turn
from green to gold to blackened night
to knowing the difference between wrong and right
and still I failed to stand and fight
in this last caress, I sharpen a sentence to slice my chest
and when I am unearthed, exposed
hope that another living breathing soul
might glimpse all that I could not say and could not show
for my final act, I should like
to call all those wasted moments back
and ask that they be buried
underneath the vaulted sky
for they deserve to be remembered
certainly not I

The Moment is Gone
Steve Wheeler

The moment is gone before
you have cause to draw breath;
it's a lost key, a forgotten
cause or another little death.

There is traffic on the road
and there is traffic in my head.
if the traffic lights aren't cycling
then I might be seeing red.

Digressing and suppressing
all my life in hexadecimal
I'm twitching like a rock star
I once saw at Reading festival.

Oh how that crowd roared out
and added to the raucous noise;
the thrashing and cacophony
boys will be boys—with toys.

That moment now is over
and I've missed the boat again;
I couldn't even capture it
with a telephoto lens.

I wish, oh how I wish, that
I could measure out those hours
in minutes and in seconds with
that bunch of stolen flowers.

But the moment passes quickly
and I fear I won't survive
if I try to turn the clock back
to September, eighty five.

22-Minute Power Cut
Ryan Morgan

The lights go out.
Let's gather about
With cheerful solidarity
In the adventurous novelty!
Huddled in our living room
As the corners close in gloom
To revel in the sudden stillness.
A perfect excuse to halt our business.
For the storm has slammed its mighty fist
On the grinding wheel of daily grist.
And now we get to stop for a while:
Just ... halt in the hop over modern life's stile
To survey the view in its natural glow,
Assay the value of a more gentle tempo.
Yes, an unexpected pause can be a rare delight
When subjected to enforced respite.
But all this is in the expectation
That there shall resume illumination
In an hour, say: no more than a day.
But suppose the cessation stays this way?
Would I feel so sanguine about the lack of supply
If the energy underpinning my life ran dry?
No, the implications are too sickly to contemplate
If electrification did not quickly reinstate.
As candles dwindled, batteries depleted,
In a shambles, crippled, quarters unheated
I would slowly fade in helplessness,
For survival training I don't possess.
Civilisation would collapse without refrigeration,
Heat, light and digital communication.
All the skill set I need for a chance to persevere
Is kept now on the internet, and would also disappear.
I can't fish, can't hunt, can't grow, can't sew.
I'd vanish 'neath the brunt of the shadow of woe.
I take as read the security of supply,
And if it went permanently dead, so would I.

Oh. It's back on.
Not a pylon black swan.
Better put the dinner on.

Lion
James Alexander Crown

As bold as the godly,
The Proverb sayeth,
Noble, royal
And strong.

Unparalleled
In stateliness,
The Revelator's
Song.

Sung out
The stony centuries,
The Root of David
Roars,

The Beast hath
Struck
Upon the heel;
The Beast can strike
No more.

Conquering Lion
Of the Tribe of Judah,
Open the
Seventh Seal.

To the Lion that is
The Lamb that was slaughtered,
All of Heaven
Kneels.

The Gap
Lorna Caizley

An iconic image grew strong, it bloomed
Seasons and moods blessed in gentle beauty.
Stood firm, branched out, with nature attuned
An ancient soldier always on duty
Prince of thieves, finding such quiet solace
Ramblers wall, follow on to the path
Lovers intent, an eternal promise
Crowds do lament, over woodcutters wrath
Gap now emptied from its stunning glory
Sycamore fell, edited forever
Many now lost a part of their story
Insanity? Or just big and clever?
Visitors lost, there was more than plenty
Can't resurrect, the gap is now empty!

Evil
Robert Atkins

While the red gobbets of the Maxim gun whistle
All day long through the sky's infinity of blue,
And while the King sends his squads of blood and gristle
To the mincer whether clad in green or red hue;

While an evil madness a hundred thousand churns
In cauldron of the war into a rancid dung;
—O, holy Mother Nature, while yet the earth turns
With summer green and joy, have mercy on the young…

There is a God who dotes on altars richly spread
With damascene, with incense-dripping golden cup
And whom the croons of choristers will butter up,

Who only wakes when mothers weeping for their dead
And doubled up in grief bring out their widow's mites
And hand them back to him a grateful sacrifice.

View from a Vase
Tom Cleary

Those bright stemmed roses
once flourishing in light yellows,
burgundy shows and orange sunglows
a bright green sheen of leaves shimmering
within sheaves of stems
now begin to curl, furling,
twirling the pearls of an older girl
no longer as elegant or awhirl
a slight stoop, the drying skin of a drooping chin
yet more intense in the faded incense
a subtle effulgence of age
as I, soon to turn the final page
seem relieved in their reprieve
from the grievous thought
of being brought to the garbage stage.
In their new community of likes
they purview and skew brighter again
among friends.

Dangling Ringlets in Spring's Hair
Sean Timms

I breathe in deeply the nectareous scents
of vibrant hues and verdigris blues
as mists of fragrant memories wear away
wisteria cascades like sweet blooms of lavender
Delicate are the drooping racemes draped
stunningly below springs sunny face
igniting a timeless grace of floral splendour
I breathe in deeply the nectareous scents
wisteria's softest shades lavender plumes
like dangling ringlets in springs hair
as zephyrs sprinkle petals below
I find myself enveloped
by ethereal beauty and redolence

Smells
Gemma Tansey

The smell of freshly baked bread, when it's only just been cooked
The smell of baby's heads, the scent of innocence I'm hooked
The smell of heavy raindrops, at the end of a day of hot sun
The smell of playdoh and paper, reminds me of childish fun

The smell of greasy hair, that makes someone smell unique
The smell of baby lotion with comfort and cleanliness speak
The smell of fabric softener all fluffy nice and clean
The smell of fresh cut grass with all its pastures green

The smell of talcum powder, shaken on freshly washed skin
The smell of lavender fields, aroma of seasons begin
The smell of clean laundry all crisp, fresh and new
The smell of cherry menthol or morning rain and dew

The smell of burning wood with a smoky chokey waft
The smell of glue and paint with which we use to craft
The smell of citrus fruit that makes your taste buds tingle
The smell of women's perfume that tends to intermingle

The smell of your pillow when it's not been washed
The smell of your partner that is never lost
The smell of old teddies that have gathered dust
The smell of old books with a hint of must

The smell of old vinyl, not like a CD
The smell of a stranger that's new to me
The smell of cigarettes that chokes the air
The smell of a woman with newly washed hair

The smell of vanilla and strawberries sweet
The smell of hash like a moreish treat
The smell of you and the smell of me
The smell of things you can't even see

The smell of the sea and the smell of spring air
The smell of fear if you really dare
The smell of joy that we cannot detect
The smells of memory that we cannot reject.

Weightless Anchor
Jou Wilder

We clang like anchors
two kilos short of five pounds.
You love me broken—
I love you barking—
a wolf in sheep's clothing.

You love me when I falter
and I love you
when your voice frays—
low and almost beautiful.

You morphed into sorrow
I never asked to hold.

I drift into you
like tide to breakwater
knowing we'll scatter—
and we'll call it closeness.

Yet we both stayed—
not because it was right.
But because we knew
no one else had learned our silence.

Digital Dementia
Iain Strachan

random tapestry of broken threads
and sputtered thoughts
let go of myhead
of dark tatty framework
random tapestry of   broken   threads
your face a putter of pixelate
of void and indescreams
who are you?
recognition degrade.
randomtapestry of   broken
fear of word salad
words wrong order in out coming
jigsaws shattered and mixed observe
*   random   tapestry*
I start a sentence and—
I start a sentence—
Frowny puzzle
I start a sen—
*   random tapès   tapes*
Your face Picasso'd
Of void cubisms
who are you?
Your face unrecog-
random   ac   cess
vile chaos of screams
the urge thoughts
memories broken jigsaw
sense encryption key
lost lost at the extremes of ideas
access de   nied
warp anything in my head
bad blocks glitch
one zero indistinct
thoughts of neurons churning
turns and Picasso
access bro   ken.   Ken?

floating think through the settle
rotting the dready against the
mental first but colours
ran   *domthreads*
symphony of failing chips
cluster of
Picasso'd
unrec-
broken   *symph-*
fade   *out*

Love Rocks
Linda Falter

You rock me, baby
You shake my soul
Love so intense
It makes me whole…
Your love is like
A lamp of gold
Shines so bright
And hot to hold…
Fire and ice
Strawberries and cream
On mountain tops
Or by a stream…
The scent of your hair
The feel of your skin
I open my heart
And let you in…
You rock me, baby
You shake my soul
Love so intense
It makes me whole…
Love Rocks …

A Poet Writes
Fouzia Sheikh

A poet writes
about truths,
what is, and what is not...
a poet writes about nature,
people, sun, moon and stars
a poet dares to feel
to see the whole world...
A poet writes..
To vent his/her own shares
of joy and agony
Aches, miseries and affection.
As well as those of the others,
A poet reads, sees through
Someone else's eyes
Face, words, voice and actions.
A poet writes
To cite reasons, so a hurting one
Would believe again.
To have faith in life, love,
Again to reach out
To those who have
Gone far in the dark.
To take them back to the fold
Of the bright side.
A poet writes
To tell the woes of those
oppressed the world over
Those tortured, violated and killed
Of children abused,
Their future stolen away from them.
A poet writes
Of how nature has been
Explained and maltreated

How human beings
Could disappear one day
How nature would be around
No matter what.
A poet is sensitive,
Observant and vigilant
A poet is compelled to see
And tell all the truth.
Truths of yesterday, those that are
Here now happening.
And those of tomorrow
And beyond all these
A poet must write
And nothing more and nothing less.

Glide
Tracey Buster & Tim Queen

leaving the ramp
he grabs
the solid air
winged with focus
time slows
and folds
plummeting
pulling gravity
perpendicular
mastering blood
and bone in empty
breath of fate
jumps as pure
as poetry
landing softly
with a plan

Acta Non Verba
Charlene Phare

Promise me no pardon
Evil has not prevailed
Confined to dark places
Conflict begins within

Speaketh of truth only
After, ill will remain
Silence from the shadows
Calming waters ripple

Acta non verba
Mighty sword withdrawn
Falling clouds echo
Laying blame as before

Pictures now frozen
Visions start to reflect
Golden sands running
Timeless hourglass shaken

Under sudden pressure
Petrol dowsing charcoal
Rapid heat rising
Moisture levels increase

Stuttered conversations
Uttered without remorse
Complex mitigation
Drama cannot reverse

Fall of a Good Man
John M. Wright

Can you see the cracks
Is it obvious
When did it start
Where does it end

A subtle descend
He was a good man
Pushed down
Counted out

Empathy overload
A push here or there
A transformation
Started with a tear
An ending with a death and
A crooked smile
A rise

There were signs
A cold heart
From ashes of apathy
A monster to arise
I am what you made me

Singular thought
Filling my head
Mindless rage
Hurt those who hurt
Your pain is my peace

Swan Song
Zac Warden

At her dressing table,
The powder sits heavy upon her brow today.
The mascara highlighting hollows,
The cruel light emphasising grey.

Damson lipstick to adorn,
Paint that which time has torn,
Pat down her dress,
Time to address,
The paying punters, ten bucks fore-sworn.

This ritual of transformation,
Honed over oh, so many years.
The highs and lows,
The critic's applause, or cause of silent tears.

Decades…
A cruel master, Fame.
Yet a lifetime she chased it,
No one else to blame.

The limelight, would burn brighter tonight,
After her final number, the curtain would rise no more.
Her voice becoming a remembered echo,
There would be no more, encore.

No time for melancholy,
For the show must go on.
She rises, resplendent,
Time for her swan song…

'No more than three months'
That's what the doctor had said.
She takes one last look in the mirror,
' come on old girl' she smiles—
'let's go knock em dead'…

A Triumph of Bees on Alkanet
Kate Cameron

Bonneville tyres,
swallow these lanes
narrow in these valleys
these old creek roads
tarmac slipping back to earth…
pasty crimped
with watery shine
you remain alert and look

I dreaming seer
how star of Bethlehem
delicately mists
purist white in elegant shine
and sun
kissed,
the picture that I didn't take
to catalogue this life,
this engine thrust

I have the mind of gleaming crows
glowing bluebells in young wet grass
I find one tiny vibrant yellow shell
fragrant violets, lime tree shadows
flickering….as we pass…

The Thought of You
Valerie Dohren

Oh, how I love the thought of you
The things you did, the things you knew
And how my heart does sing with praise
As I recall those magic days

Those magic days when first we met
Such days I never shall forget
When love was young, and we were too—
The sun rose high, the sky turned blue

The sky turned blue, the stars shone bright
Each day was warm, and warm each night—
The days and nights became as one
As did all time beneath the sun

Beneath the sun our love was born
Then nurtured by the golden dawn
And oh how sweet that magic world
Wherein true love became unfurled

True love became unfurled, so sweet
Like nectar in the summer's heat
But oh too soon the years have flown
With you now gone and I, alone

And I, alone, am left to weep
To steal each day and steal my sleep—
Remembering the days we knew,
Oh, how I love the thought of you

Isles of Love
Brandon Adam Haven

Shuddering shores of your crimson wail,
Ire birthing in soft, seraphic sanguine.
Unbind to thrash and set sail
As we venture, glittering gleam
Through the malodorous waters of sea.
Our toes dipped in searing aureate,
Where we glance candidly the isles of love.

Branded fondly in old man's visions,
We ascend the loathsome derision
To find what has become so lost.
But fearfully, the soul is the cost,
Branched upon a forgotten shelf
In a rainy merchant's bloom,
Waiting to again be held.

January Day
Joan Audette

Don't leave my heart hanging
on this January day
like laundry frozen to the line

Like a shivering sparrow
looking for crumbs,
how long do I linger and wonder

Will I ever see your face at the door?
Your smile like a beam of sunshine,
warm through the wintry pane

The Cross
Ian Cave

It was a fair trade,
in the nineties,
Ethiopian crafts
to alleviate famine.

We have owned it for decades,
hanging at the top of the stairs,
stepping past every day,
with hardly a glance.

Today, I see it with new eyes,
a passing comment,
lamenting the pain and suffering
of humanity on the cross.

The cross I see is different:
a dark lattice embroidered on white linen,
connecting matter with the eternal,
the beauty in mortal kind.

Being, shaping the universe
with intricate design,
the people's path following songlines,
framing the concept of life.

Threads of red, green and gold
interlace the cross,
ribbons flowing from the heart
to the earth below.

The deep red of blood,
pulsing with life,
returning to the ground,
to be welcomed by death.

The verdant green of flora,

transforming the light
into the deep matrix of forest,
the lush herbage of pasture.

The shining allure of gold,
the wealth of life,
flowing from the distant star,
flowering in natural beauty.

The theme repeated
in a tree of life,
the fruits of mortality
crowning the cross.

The four elements
frame the linen,
reflected in divine sunlight,
a shroud to hold the gift of life.

It is a fair trade
in a modern day,
seeing something new
in what you had all along.

Necromancing
Jamie Willis

There are no skeletons in my closet
They're on full display, and wildly dancing
I've maybe kept a soul two
Locked in vials, tucked away
Next to all the letters
That I wrote when life had sweet romancing
I check on them from time to time
Inhale the memories, til I feel better
Truthfully, I think they like it
Being conjured when I choose
I pull their silver cords my way

Across the astral, while I play
With all the things we stood to lose
And how I never want to stay
I cork the graves, content to pine
—only when I'm necromancing
Then I'm off to dance with Grimm
on a full moon Saturday.

A Walk through Silence
Tom Watkins

The Finnish forest whispers "Come in"
The silence welcomes you

The snow beneath my feet
crunches and squeaks
The spiralling pines sway
creating white noise and creaks
releasing an earthy fragrance to enjoy

My cadence and breath
become my metronome
Trees rubbing together in the wind
Woodpecker taps a melody
Squirrel scurries up a tree

The soft wiping of my dripping nose
The nothingness of the falling snow

The rapid thump, thump
of my galloping heart
The warmth of the cold breeze
My personal thoughts
hold me in the moment

I was welcomed to the Finnish forest
and not disappointed by the silence

Endless Possibilities
Emile Pinet

From the ashes of despair,
embers flare into anger.
And gnawing pangs of hunger
force the soul to question sin.

No matter what you believe,
only death offers release.
And there are no exceptions
to this universal truth.

Although lechers purchase flesh,
Hypocrisy sets the price.
For lust's an expensive dish;
served with a smidgen of shame.

Intermingled in purpose;
Hope's a catalyst for faith.
And morphs into the role of
wish-giver and dream builder.

Love is undefinable;
and yet undeniable.
Residing in the realm of
endless possibilities.

Layers
Zac Warden

I sit silently
Below an opaque film
Unseen.
I was once bright,
Bordering on garish.
Long limbed branches,
Host to exotic
Multi coloured birds, from far flung lands.
Flamboyant was I.
I was grandeur.
I was decadence.
My opulent presence demanding attention,
Dominating the room.
All other adornments
But Mere trinkets.
The furniture sat in reverent servitude of my art.
Purchased to compliment
My very existence.
The pinnacle of extravagance,
Of indulgence,
Of sophistication and taste.
An unapologetic display of wealth and standing.
Of class and the times.
But time marches on…
The years passed by,
The sunlight unkind in its
Bleaching of my colours.
Still yet was I resplendent,
The focal point of the room.

Fashions changed.
My attendants replaced.
With furnishings in keeping with new times.
Yet I endured still,
Although now a quirky backdrop.
Rather than the showpiece I once was.

Niche, unique,
Still remarkable,
Still a talking point
Until....
Alas infamy!
A usurper mounted upon my beautiful face.
A dirty blot upon my vista.
A gag to my visual song.
Am I now an embarrassment to be muted so?
I am wronged! Suddenly inconspicuous in plain sight
Second fiddle
To this soulless magic box
Of flickering hypnotic light!
That sucks in all consciousness...
silently I weep in my humiliation.
Then the fateful day.
White sheets spread over the sparse
now minimalistic furniture.
At least my companions were not witness to my demise.
Nor voyeur to my censure.
The smell of paint, the sense of my obliteration.
As the first cold strokes of a roller sent shock through me.

My birds of paradise erased
My reaching boughs shorn.
Fauna and flora eradicated.
Until stifled,
I was no more.
I am here still.
Although not.
Backstage,
Supporting role to the beige
Taste of today.
Or magnolia if you prefer
Cruelly humbled,
Made invisible and
bitter in my isolation.
As irrelevant as the
Wall paper, that in turn lies beneath me.
Forgotten...

What Happiness is
Ashly Tenini

Happiness is—
Laughter in the rain, dogs in the sunlight,
A moment of calm, a day without pain.

Happiness is—
A snow cone melting in sticky, sweet delight,
A slushy in hand on a blazing summer night,
Jumping in the pool, first splash of the season,
No questions asked, no need for a reason.

Happiness is—
Watching your child as she learns and grows,
Loving her more than she'll ever know.
The way her smile rewrites your day,
Innocence blooming in every way.

Happiness is—
Waking up to wet noses and wagging tails,
To a love that lingers, never fails.
To feeling close to something wide and deep—
To God, to grace, to promises we keep.

Happiness is everywhere—
In fragments of light, in a quiet embrace.
We just must notice it,
And hold it eternally in its place.

Poet's Teatime
Neil Mason

Oh to be in England
Now my boiled egg is ready
Into the valley of the shadows of death
Rode the brave six hundred bread soldiers
Stands the church clock at ten to three
Applauding the cucumber sandwiches arrival
"how charming and sweet you sing"
I said to the boiling headed kettle
While brushing a few commas from the tablecloth
Poets teatime in HD sound and vision
Sentences with crusts neatly cut off
Cakes sliced into a mouth of words
And for that moment a blackbird sang
Poets teatime curtains with pencil precision drawn
Verses slept in warm lyrical paragraphs

Blurred Image
Joan Audette

Your face is blurred as I gaze through the window of my mind
How can that be, when oh so many times
I traced your features with my fingertips
Touched them with my lips
Re-lived them in my dreams

I strain to focus now as on a faded photograph
Is it merely the tears in my eyes
Or has so much time passed
that your image is now obscure?

And is there a chance we might meet again
on the winding paths of our separate and uncertain lives?

The Merry Maidens
Ian Cave

Hand in hand, we approach the dancing stones.
"Widdershins or Turnwise?" The eternal question.
I choose Turnwise, looking to the future.
We weave between the stones,
Firm in their resolve.
We kiss as we turn, offering the opposite hand.
We begin to smile, seeing our future,
One stone at a time,
Holding our promise with the next kiss.
Our smiles turn to laughter,
Our hearts lifting with the release of time.
We complete the circle, find its center,
To hold our love.

Searching my eyes, you ask me
What it all means.
Our love enacted, made firm as the stones.
I return the question, closing the circle
As I roll head over heels
To land at your feet.
"I don't deserve you."
Widdershins or Turnwise?
You decide.

Where have I held your hand?
Kevin Francis

Where have I held your hand?
Through long haul flights
On Caribbean walks
In Dublin bars
And late night cars
Where have l held your hand?
On sunset boulevard

London shows
Overnight stays
And busy days
Where have I held your hand?
Through wedding vows
And Family rows
Some wonderful sights
And mountain heights
Where have I held your hand?
As machine sensors beep
Watching you sleep
By your bedside all night
Watching you fight
...To live

Name That Movie
Patrick Darnell

Rose Sayer: *'I never dreamed that any mere physical experience could be so stimulating."*

I've been part of this group for nine years
I've observed it evolve and roil in its own pot liquors
I dressed up in my buckskin shreddies
I put Pink Floyd on as I got ready
But I wrote nothing as great as this line for Rose Sayer.

Yes, not one line out of many have I written for show
Encapsulates the hurry-scurry of post orgasmic afterglow
As this bit of script, delivered by Kate,
At the climax of the scintillating escape,
Yes, to match this wit, I must dig deeper with foot and elbow.

Yield, knuckle under, move over, eat the stover,
Be clever, be nice, forage the Dutch clover
I will not give up nor tarry at the bar
I will not drink to the lowness of Kishar
Of this word herd I'll be once and forever its drover.

Through the Tears
Eric Aguilar

An old soul sung
to the tune of new woes.
A tongue too stung
by words uncontrolled.

Life's bitter taste in
wastelands of what I seek.
Discouraged at the loss
of things I think I need.

Working out the issues
between courage and fear,
at times you feel so far but,
in silence you are near.
So disobedient of what you ask,
and yet you still appear.
It was you who wiped my eyes
and took me through the tears.

My life a sinners test,
at my best, I still fail.
In a tantrum like an infant,
tears streaming as I wail.

You take the pain, grief, and anger
into the depths of seeds sown.
I emerge with new growth
of things I've never known.

Working out the issues
between courage and fear,
at times you feel so far but,
in silence you are near.
So disobedient of what you ask,
and yet you still appear.
It was you who wiped my eyes
and took me through the tears.

You shake and move circumstance
to correct all the problems
and lovingly intercede
with the answers to solve 'em.

And, I may not always like
the way that things may go
but, I will trust in you,
the keeper of my soul.

Working out the issues
between courage and fear,
at times you feel so far but,
in silence you are near.
So disobedient of what you ask,
and yet you still appear.
It was you who wiped my eyes
and took me through the tears.

Dove Cottage
Alan Sharkey

A look into the past
An honour abound
A vision of serenity
All around
Of tiny clogs
And tiny gowns
Of darkness and light
And slate to the ground
Of parties and laughter
With friends around
A humble abode
With love to be found
Just half a moon
To show off the ground
A trickle of water
The only sound

Look Up and See, Believe You can be Free

Shirley Rose

So envious of clouds in the sky who roam free and travel anywhere in the world can hang high or low huge or tiny any color from black to white purple orange red even green can be any size they want to be from tiny cotton ball to horizon-to-horizon wall with powers magnificent even sometimes malevolent producing destructive killing storms spitting out bolts of electricity what power (or a gentle morning shower) a huge deluge to scour the face of the earth the clouds can even block out the light of day and the lights of night no celestial bodies can be seen if clouds are feeling really mean but sometimes they just romp and play like little girls on a Summer day floating free letting themselves be stretched in the breeze trying on various tresses even choosing rainbows as dresses a cloud just is it has no worries nor any stresses just water vapor and a bit of dust maybe snow and ice in Winter climes a cloud should remind us of us how fleeting and fragile and temporary our time we need to chill we need to float no need to gloat or compare with our kin because we are all the same under the skin just air just thin so paper-thin a fleeting thought a whimsy a whim play-things on a huge game board meant to delight and entertain the Creator of all Almighty Lord!

A Fool's Message
Leslie Clark Hicks

I sometimes wonder where I might
be
    without the ability to see what is before
me;   glimpses of
shadows behind
me...
    ~echoes of
memories~
                erased to protect—mayhap trickery of
spirituality!
                Lost in imbalances of thought;
a glimpse of dimensions
    not meant to be seen
...
                a fool's message can be
bought
        if one remains weak—in
thought!
    Signs all
around
                —shards of
synchronicities
                ignite what embodies the
soul,
    as the Universe pulsates ...a Oneness within.

A Maritime Hymn
Joseph Deal

Dead Sailors
Wail sad songs,
              Sung
Like bells tolled
From silent wrecks keeled deep
In the cold cathedral
Of the dark Atlantic—

Held down by their throats,
By the frigid fingers of
Maritime waters,
Among the ribs
Of their tossed ship.

Their ghostly grip
Heave and haul on ropes
Now rigged on masts
In salty depths.

If you listen carefully,
You can hear their
Sad chorus capsized
As flotsam
In the surf—

Muted hymns
Rolling off their tongues in
Waves whispering of their
Tragic fate—
Finally reaching the
                      Shore.

Nothing More to Lose
Emile Pinet

As shadows shift and day departs
Dusk bruises the sky, black and blue.

And like a billion bleeding hearts,
Sol absorbs a bright scarlet hue.

Infidelity's surreal,
severing your heart in mid-beat.

And although his love isn't real,
leaving is a difficult feat.

Wounded feelings fester within
as the sun abandons the sky.

For tomorrow, cannot begin
with the words of a whispered lie.

Filling your heart with fear and dread,
depression and anger compete.

And reflecting on what was said,
exposed his level of deceit.

You cannot say why love didn't last,
so you question your heart for clues.

For all your dreams lie in the past,
and now, you've nothing more to lose.

Bee and Snowdrop
Richard Harries

A snowdrop, a symbol of Spring
Of renewal, white, bright, pure
Thrusting strong and straight out of the earth
The circle of life
The changing of the seasons
The plant's promise to renew
To survive
From bulb to flower and back again
A bee, a symbol of renewal
Of life and fertilization
And a threat, not to the planet
(The planet will survive)
But mankind may not
If we exterminate the bee
Pollination will not happen
Mankind will not eat
We will be the ones to starve, to die
Here we have them joining together
Here we have them within one image
An image of beauty and hope
Yes hope
Hope for the survival of mankind
If we were to learn
And ensure our survival

Summer Shine
Neil Mason

The morning rises early
Long before birds whistle up a dawn chorus
A sun reaches out to the world in a warm and friendly manner
The flower garden opens up as it were a book
Leaves and petals are words that everybody reads
Knowledge is a fragrant breeze firing the writers creativity
Busy bees working their magic in blue sky scenery
Summer shine bright as sunflower coins
Days seem everlasting
The way it should be
Love is a summer fruit bowl igniting loving taste buds
Summer shine is a mirror in life's future

Mirror of Truth
Archie Papa

I'm the uncontrollable variant
appearing as I see fit
exposing flawed opinions
disguised as sarcastic wit
My gravity attracted wisdom
my insight worthy of belief
accept in me to understand
or deny me in tears of grief
Overseeing the happenstance
listening to every word
honesty speaks a language
the deceitful have never heard
Reality is viewed in my light
my energy cannot be destroyed
kindness gains to trust in me
so hatred cannot fill the void
Reflected in you, the innocence of youth
gaze in our eyes, the mirror of truth

Water Pearls
Gayle-Anne Hart

Water pearls running
Like a silent stream
Down from my fingertips
Making paths across my palms
Cool and fresh across my skin
Like glistening translucent pearls
Running down to the edge of hands
Flowing off like small waterfalls
Falling and splashing
From where they come.

Hats Off
J. Henry DeKnight

Battery acid burn
   when will I ever learn
keep to myself
mouth shut
　singed with a chemical cut

Stagger around in the dark
  like drunk balancing on a mark
gluing the pieces that somehow remain
   driving slow in the fast lane

Trigger the weapon of truth
   a martini without vermouth
 a bullet slow as a snail
    drinking from life's cocktail

When will I ever learn
just sitting back waiting my turn
  silent like feral cat
to you I tip my hat

Dear Mind
Amanda Mtshulana

Dear mind, you've wandered far,
Through thoughts and dreams like a distant star,
You've chased the shadows and danced with fears,
And searched for answers through all tears.

You've held the memories of joy and pain,
And kept the secrets that you'd rather not explain,
You've been the witness to every rise and fall,
And guided me through the darkness, night's dark wall.

Dear mind, you're weary from the constant strife,
The endless questions the search for life,
But still you ponder and still you seek,
The meaning of it all the mysterious unique.

So rest now, dear mind and let the calm descend,
Let go of me worries and let peace attend,
Find the stillness you'll find your way,
And in the quiet, a brighter dawn will stay.

Mood Swings
Terry Bridges

Interstices in twinkling inner light
Private dreads and dreary personal black holes
The fearsome memory and symmetry of terror
Past errors multiply increase arithmetically
A pathetic abacus counts down reminiscent hours with beads
Terminal horror in the night's oblique stare
Hope is a whopping whore's luxury of thought
Brain-dead dawn reverses and curses
Sucks and swallows like a monolithic mouth
The mad moon the dying stars the bleak coal sky
I hesitate between the cracks of bliss and fury
A universal metronome vibrates in solid air

4 am
Alan Sharkey

The dawn moon rises above Morecambe Bay.
Majestic in its arrogance.
Sitting proudly as if to say.
Ignore me? You've got no chance.
Pastel shades cover the sky.
Artists urged to replicate.
A stone circle of days gone by.
The ghost of a celebrated saint.
How can I leave this place?
A home I've made my own.
A lifetime torn with such disgrace.
To venture out alone.
To chase a dream long since held.
A chance to start again.
To leave the hills and endless fells.
A cloak to shield the pain.

So to all Barrovians I say.
Revel in its glory.
I may return to you one day.
With a whole new different story.

Una Vita
Trude Foster

One life,
one light to shine in our allotted hour
a single strutting chance upon the stage
a single line writ large upon the page,
a chance to love, to live, to give
and what is more,
one entrance and one exit, no encore

Tears from the Sun
Peter Rivers

The sun carries sorrow
As if it's being chased by tomorrow
A nose bleed panic attack fight
Hidden in plain sight behind bright daylight

If I talked to a nighthawk what would it say?
Would it smile then speak of shadow
Invading the light even during the day…
Thoughts only wisdom can know

Clouds commit crime casting bruises across your shine
Truly how high does this corruption go?
What does the evidence show?
Conspiracies from the people
who make a dime off daylight savings time

What does it symbolize when the sun is noon high
but the sky begins to cry?
Every sun shower that lasts a minute or an hour
Has special power to amplify the light of the moon
A world of refracting reflection
in droplet sized glimmering eyes
Telling the daylight "I'll see you soon"

Obsessed
Janette Curran

I am yearning for the contact.
Your hand tracing my neck
Running down my back and around my waist
To wrap my arms around you tightly
Feel your heartbeat and mine race
To have you back where you need to be

A Decade Passed
Lorna Caizley

Time it tumbles forward,
A decade somehow passed.
Feels like only yesterday
Since we saw you last.

Memories crumble backwards
When you spring to mind.
Though life, it's sometimes fractured
It's on days like this we pine.

In hope, you see the moments
Transcribed throughout our days
The mirror image components
Still within the summer rays

Your wisdom, it still guides us
Through panic and through grace
We'll always be reminded
Of the love within your face.

When Stars they Whisper
Matthew Burgio

When stars they whisper in the night,
They whisper of the love we share,
And even Cupid feels the spite
When stars they whisper in the night.
For oft they twinkle white and bright,
Though one might pause and find it rare
When stars they whisper in the night.
They whisper of the love we share.

I Have Walked
J. P. Hayter

I have walked all over England,
And it seems old England has walked all over me!
Like a map, the heart lights up its secret ways,
pumps its life force that threads me to existence,
My memory is filled with
a deep melancholic yearning,
For it seems I have walked all over England,
and old England has walked all over me!
Every recollection,
Is a sickness, a nostalgia,
a fever that possesses me!
It tramples on my dreams, and shows me
somewhere else I'd like to be !
For I know beneath the bow of the old oak tree,
And in the hollow of the hidden valley
is somewhere where you kissed me,
Now I weep, for the old England
I did walk over cares not for me!
I hear its echoes in the bracken
and in the laughter of the babbling brook,
The birdsong,
Mocking me,
Forsaken love, carried on the wind it laments,
the time that rushes by,
For all I have is England,
And my soul grows ever weary of its song,
As if it's also mocking me,
England that tramples me under foot,
In it's unforgiving recollections, its hamlets,
bells and country lore,
I am misunderstood!

I Dance with the Darkness
Jennifer M. Nichols

Entangled,
in the interlude of dreaming,
disquietude invades this
loathsome imposter
and skulks from my being…
Like some clandestine voyeur,
I dance with the darkness,
stripped and bare,
standing on the precipice,
between light and dark,
betwixt life and death.

Striving to suppress
the shapeless murkiness
of unforgiving dysphoria,
dark reflections
overshadow
rose-tinted versions
of acceptability, and
I weep from within…
my shameful silhouette,
filled with fear,
vicariously evokes resolution,
and sequesters in the shadows,
should night's lustre
enunciate this infidelity…

Prophecies for the Age of Indifference
Michael Hukkanen

Raised, as I was,
on a diet
of low-fiber religion
and fast food education
how healthy can I be
when nothing matters
I struggle to withdraw
so there I went, spent
bedraggled and fading
sodden with disbelief
into the desert, like
some mystic of self-destruction
the poet child of in between
who, blinded, seeks visions
within the little deaths
prophecies for
the age of indifference
Deprived of food
and slumber
love and shelter
safety and belief
I suffer scorching days
endless freezing nights
to rise, once again,
empty handed
save the memory of magic
a butterfly, pinned down
with words, wings spread
crucified

O, Poetry
Karin J. Hobson

Take by brush one dab at a time
and scent of oil in a lesser air;
Gently swoosh-paint on palette of mine
And, I to you shall aptly apply on and on
~
Swab caressing on canvas of white
'fore Helios hails a star-strewn nite;

At which time I shall ungate,
Cypress shadow-shaded palisade;
Whereupon Tuscany views propagate
ethereal visions of Heavenly Grace
~
How do you build a ladder to the skies
Without wisps of poetic why not, whys?

O, Poetry thou art brush and stroke
Painted hues that, if acclaimed, evoke;
O, fanciful words to go as far as
mind ajar traversing tenebrous Stars!
~
And, dare glints blink and eye fade
Raise up thy pen, and to thine I say,

"O, bring on effulgent glow of he,
to Eternity I shall indeed find she!"

Weather
Terry Bridges

This hour is elastic and lasts too long
Anticipating the juggernaut of doom
I pace around the room like marathon-man
One step forward two steps back
Circling my tracks in a planetary motion
Emotions gravitate me into temporary orbit
I steam along huffing and puffing
This ticker was always dodgy territory
I feel the heartbeat of an alien world
Pulse in this crenelated steely brain
A storm unnamed though hurricane force
I batten down my thoughts into a meditation
The course of my actions like a snail's silver slime
Crawling into a shining future...my panic behind

The Stitch
Joseph Deal

As we slit the stitch
That draws our eyes together
And part our gaze to separate ways
The thread in the seam
Of sheer cloth that binds us
For these brief moments
Pull me apart as you leave.

I dash frantically
Grasping at the pieces
Of fine line
Hand over hand—
Trying to pull you back,
But as I unravel
I'm left standing here—
Undone.

The Wild
Anna Treasure

One day
I tried to outrun
The Wild.
I was 12.

I couldn't do it.
Even with arms
like streamers and
wind on cheeks

the yearning still
pulled. Unfulfilled,
I sat and cried
under the silver
Spruce fir tree.

I realised then
The time of loving
till it hurt and hating
till it hurt more
was going to end.
It had to.

Running headlong
into the wind is too
dangerous in the
adult world where
words reign
supreme.

The passion of
The Wild and
such things as
love and hate
are swaddled
with words.

I didn't know
that then.
All I felt was
a looming loss.
I hadn't outrun

The Wild, and
soon it would be
eclipsed by
the mess of
adulthood.

The Shadow of Yesterday
Valerie Dohren

I am the shadow of yesterday
holding fast to the far horizon—
yet slipping away, beyond the edge of time.
I embrace each memory, and enshroud
all hopes and dreams, soon to be lost
beyond the capture of today.

I am the shadow of yesterday
holding fast to the far horizon—
yet fading away, with the coming dawn.
I carry with me all of my existence
counting each precious moment, soon to be lost
beyond the capture of today.

I am the shadow of yesterday
holding fast to the far horizon—
afraid to let go of all that I own and treasure.
But, I see you there waiting for me
coming out of the darkness, soon to be lost
beyond the capture of today.

Under a Different Circumstance
Graeme Stokes

I'd run a marathon of gauntlets,
for your smile at the finishing line
Any lost cause you had support it,
until I died I'd get behind
For any whim that swims deep water,
any fancy that floats your boat
I'd make come true if I could court ya,
lay beside your beating pulse
I'd risk it all without hesitation,
fill the pot with every chip
To have that blissful moist sensation,
of my soul stuck to your lips
If you would just grant me a window,
I'd fly through as you advanced
I'd sleep soundly on my pillow,
under a different circumstance

I'd sail every big harsh ocean,
if when I docked I met your eyes
My spirits would dance the locomotion,
from your laugh's daily supply
Every night would be like Christmas,
as I watched you while you dreamed
I'd never tire or grow listless,
of ever listening to you breathe
To sense our bond through entwined fingers,
your electrifying charge
At the door of your thoughts I'd linger,
'till you opened up your heart
My whole would dive in from head to feet,
just given half the chance
Sated, my world would spin complete,
under a different circumstance

Tranquility
Simon Drake

I didn't take much to rattle my cage
It didn't take much to unlock the rage
Just a few verses written by you
Lines filled with lies not one ounce of truth
Obviously purposefully out there like bait
All you had to do was patiently wait
Curiosity stupidly got the better of me
Reeled in on your lines from the depths of tranquility
Feelings, wounds still tender to touch
Thoughts overwhelming, it's all been too much
I only have one heart and I gave it to you
Without stipulations this much is true
You shattered that heart, my hopes and my dreams
Unpicked my emotions
so they'd come undone at the seams
Tempered with evidence planted the gun
Not an iota of remorse for what you have done
Cleverly removed yourself from the scene of the crime
Then watch me take the fall knowing I'd do hard time
I hope it was worth it I hope you are pleased
To see me destroyed, on my hands and knees
I have no idea if I can rise and survive
My foolish heart wants our love revived
I deal in hard facts and actual truth
And despite your behaviour
I will only ever love you

Promises Broken
Jennifer M. Nichols

Wind whips
a million powdery pin pricks
to flail skin from the bones
of this shivering wreck,
that was once
my body...
like a marauding pirate,
you invaded me,
tortured me,
with promises,
and pledges of love...
and when I cried
at the thought of you leaving,
you told me
that you never would...
you promised,
that my heart was safe,
never again to be tossed about
on a tumultuous and turbulent ocean...
you would be my life raft...
you promised,
we were unsinkable,
'Like the Titanic',
you said...
but you are gone...
vanished into horizon's veil
of promises broken...

You're in My Arms
David Catterton Grantz

When chaos wears you like Satan's jagged cape,
When you find yourself flailing,
and there seems no escape,
Come on over, darlin' we will ballyhoo and shout
And don sweet Aretha's soul, and dance it all about.

We're not meant to bear these burdens all alone;
Come from your nautilus,
we'll stand at each other's throne.
No tyrant's gonna bring us down,
Nor his vigilantes hid around the town.
You're in my arms tonight.

A little bit of kindness goes a long, long way.
Don't give into fear, not tomorrow or today.
We'll put the rabble back into the fire;
We'll find the falconer and unspin his gyre.

Our love is bound to take us to our final rest,
Your hair of ebony, spread soft across my chest.
Our bodies speak the mysteries in our genes,
As our minds define what freedom really means.

You know love is strongest when it comes in danger,
When hate and choler ride the misdeeds of strangers;
Stay with me, love, and we'll find our way through;
You'll be with me, and I'll be here with you.

But if in the end they catch me and take me far away.
My final thought will be of you, high above the fray:
That you were in my arms this night,
This shape of you, my final sight.

Easyspeak
Gregory Richard Barden

so ...
demanding
she told me to stop
to stop 'thinking like a poet' ...
but what the hell did that mean?
she added unto, thusly—
'stop creating Tolkien worlds' (verbatim)
that hit home ...

any other fool with a pen
would take it as compliment
but I knew her too well ...
I knew *exactly* what she meant
and kindness was not the dish being served
'you are not so tragic as you think,'
she informed me
'not so heartsick as your dragon kingdoms' ...
'or their celibate heroes' ...

(my vision and ire, flooding red)
but I *am* a poet, you see
not by choice or motive
or even pitiful circumstance
and 'twas so *easy* for her to say
as my heart thrummed for naught but *her*
and her heart thrummed ...
for *him*

For So Long have I Yearned
Linda Adelia Powers

Pure spirit above the horizon dreaming
A chimera seen and seeing auroral scenes
Beaming star of morn, eclipsing dragons,
Flowing in all directions toward forgiveness,
Dissolutions, resolutions of sticky rainbows,
Enduring joy the sun and moon are loyal
Only shadow casters in passing leaving
Nothing forever frozen on the ground

Prone to superstitious cowardice
Simple goose flapping below the horizon
Neither seen or seeing imago self
Dusk and stars threaten to forget the sun
Eclipse the soul in visible exhalations
Wondering if trapped beneath a rainbow
Heady headstrong heart stuck struck
Optimistic by the steady insistence of life
Avoiding what must be done, forgetting all
Before something falls befalls, studying
Stick figure shadows left on the ground
Friends the sun and moon shine past

A train sits on the horizon
Awaiting the next rail and spike to be laid
To plow onward seeking a golden link
On giddy parallels seeing forever forward
For chances seen for catching space
Curving for majestic tristes of fate
Still asking, am I parallel to my future
Rebel, it is not my doom to swoon before
Looming years, to wash wish all time each day
Unable to build tracks much less stations
I'll pump the top of the sky for answers
Elated by the endless pounding questions
Whiling away the sunlight wheeling

Tinea
Trude Foster

A day escapes the sticky womb of night
held firm in the arms of a midwife morning
listen to its infant cries,
the wails of a newborn child unfed
demanding of your bed and sleepy scant attention,
it matters not that you turn your back and try to block your ears
to tears of open-window traffic rage
and screaming gulls that dance on bins with shoes of lead
invade your head and work themselves within
to violate your peace with a surgeon's skill,
phone alarm vibrating shrill and shaking
leaking decibels that penetrate each waking fibre of your skin
you know you must begin, attend that fractious babe
fill its hungry mouth to stop the bawling
lured as ever by the bathroom light
Thursday screams, and you her faithful moth come crawling

Night Watch
R. David Fletcher

The night shines its light on this page,
Its song a mirror of my beginnings,
Whose metaphor makes my life a stage,
My identity, shaped in endless screenings.
Now treading on this creaking floor,
Among the beams of memory's shelves,
Knotted thoughts through timeline doors,
Splintered ways, shards of myself.

Inversions
Angela Brown

Eyes aimed low
like the sullen, slow
strike of a cello bow—
with hazel-lit pitch.

Her strike is precise,
and still, inside
she quivers—
a homeless-heart-harmony,
tragic and beautiful,
dark and full of holes,
pin-pricks stitched
across her skin
like tiny stage lights.

Her bow bends to no one.

She's an aphotic elegy,
a collection of fixed measures
poured out before me.
A decrescendo glows
while she fights the strings
that still sting her…

    Still…
a faint fugue grows in her little girl soul—
a progeny of cadence
where all origin disappears
and a new movement becomes composed:

    She lets me hold her close,
    as the curtains close.

Changing Seasons
Donna Smith

Yellow corona
In unison swaying free
Narcissus in bloom

An apricot sky
Descending in the gloaming
Orange soda orb

Bare branches exposed
A garland of golden leaves
Aureate carpet

Powder ice crystals
Cascading in the crisp air
Alabaster frost

Love, Not Love
Richard de Bulat

Love's desire, keen edged between dread and hope,
Love, not love, enduring, obsessive conceit,
Something that fills the unfilling inside;

Love demanding, acquisitive, possessed;
Requited, unrequited, feeding need,
Giving one's best, rather less for taking,

But love I give, to take, make, reciprocate.
Tenderly render, lovingly dedicate.

No Skeleton is made of Gold
Jessica Ferreira Coury Magalhães

We all look the same in death
No matter if rich or poor
Famous or obscure
At the prime of the youth, or grey and old.
No amount of money or beauty
will come to your aid once you cross the threshold.
We all look the same in death
Because no skeleton is made of gold.

We all look the same in death
No amount of power can change that fact
No connections, no bribery, no strings pulled
Can alter what is about to unfold
No man can deceive death, as foretold
And no skeleton is made of gold.

You can try and cheat the living
But not the spiritual world
No plastic surgery, veneers, creams and potions
Will be of use once you abandon this earth
No blackmail, no payoff—death is not corrupt.

It is no use feeling like you are superior
It is futile to strike your best pose
When the light is out and the curtains close
You'll look just like the beggar from the street
you once scorned and rebuffed.
Sooner or later you will find out
That no skeleton is made of gold.

Pressing Petals
Chuck Porretto

Upon a rose, a thorn will lay,
the rose it does not fret.
But when the rose is in decay,
the thorn is sharper yet.
-

When may a favored flower fade,
a choice is ours to make.
To pine behind a palisade,
or press against the ache.
-

We pull the blossom from the vase,
between the pages pressed.
And now the petals take their place
as moments laid to rest.
-

With hushed horizons still asleep,
I set out from my home.
And wandered through the forest deep,
where I am wont to roam.
-

I passed into a narrow dale
within the crowded wood.
And there beneath a misty veil,
a single flower stood.
-

Juxtaposed against the pine
this blossom should not be.
But nonetheless I saw it shine,
and blooming just for me.
-

Scarlet red and violet blue,
with another snowy white.
As velvet drops of opaled dew
reflected scattered light.
-

Little flower all alone

what brings you to this place?
Perchance your seed divinely sown,
to glint of godly grace.
-
With solemn silence unrestrained,
the time was standing still.
I pondered questions unexplained,
beside the sylvan rill.
-
If I had gone another way,
would you be ever here?
Or did you blossom on this day,
because I ventured near?
-
Oh, why is this the path I crossed
while others I have missed?
And is the reason I am lost,
the reason you exist?
-
The answer I shall never know
but matter it does not.
For I will always love you so,
for joy that you have wrought.
-
I thank the Lord to let me find
this beauty rare and deep.
To press your petals in my mind,
where they shall ever keep.

When may a favored flower fade,
a choice is ours to make.
To scorn the thorn, the flower made
or keep a softer sake.
-
Upon a rose, a thorn will lay,
the flower perched above.
A thorn shall never hold my sway,
the blossom is my love.

Somewhere
John C. Algar

Somewhere,
between the words
and where years passed by,
the who we were that day we spoke—
was it smoke that teared our eyes
in later years,
or friendship gone awry?

I looked at messages sent by you,
and [in] those replies from me I sent,
we spoke of family—
yours and mine, 'n' all our doglets [too],
and trees so big no house could fill,
marrying paintings of life—so still
of what had been; but eons ago.

And when I learned,
heard all that had befallen you,
the shit that some—
one moreso in particular,
although the other one—
(a curse upon their heads
for what they, and maybe others, did to you),
I determined I'd never be as such;
for I would be a fool
to mistreat the one
who means so much to me!

But now I feel as though I've let you down,
the clown I am with so sad eyes,
the tears I cry for where we are—but now
—and I wonder; do you care for me
as I do for you?
Do you see us in the sunset,
walking there—hand in hand—
two shadows seen upon the ground
now melded into one?

Still Emitting Light
Dabendra Sahu

I remember, when I was in your womb
You used to walk daily in the frail evenings
At the bank of a lake sitting on a rock close by

To show me moon's smiles shining on water, timeless and shy
Often lying on a mat during the solitary nights
On the terrace, showed me the sky and infinite stars
As if, me able to hear, whispered their names and parables
Later often took me to the garden in your arms
Told me to touch the flowers, feel the delight of petals
Watch the rapture of the bees and the butterflies.
Also, often you took me to the balcony covered with rails
To show the nests of the little birds hanging from boughs
Peeping and chirping, their hunger to strive and survive.
A few years later, when I grew up to be an adolescent
As if you too turned young and adolescent, with me ran
Behind the brace of joyous and quacking ducks
Running into the lake waters flapping their wings.

Time has flown like river water taking you into the sea
No more you are lying on an armchair, a piece of tapestry
Smiling at me through sparkle of your flickering eyes
Never bothering about toothless lips or shivering limbs
Fragile body wrapped in shawl, feet dangling over the floor
A tacit message or indication that don't you bother
I will be around, though deep down the soil or any element
Dimensions may change but domain of heart will remain constant.

Today when I linger at the lake during the evenings
I don't see the moon reflecting on water, but you,
When I go to the terrace, I don't see the stars, but you.

When I go to the garden, I don't feel the flowers or petals
Even the bees or the butterflies no more hover over, but you.
I don't see the ducks giggling and scampering into waters, but you
I don't see the nests swinging or chicks peeping on boughs, but you.

You seem to be everywhere, a ubiquitous, in my brain,
In my breath, in my thoughts and in my being
Though time has stubbed out the wick off the table
But still lights emitting, radiating off the burn out candle.

you resemble a rapture I read
Matt Elmore

you resemble a rapture I read
ripped red eyed tired of ill failing fires
rescued from ailing under your wet rainbow arch
a sunflower resuscitated in marked green pastures
orange ya starting to feel really renewed?
fruit among fruits sweet as a magenta morning
melting like honey golden kisses on lonely lips
yellow without vitamin D from D rising sun
of love trembling in psychedelic kaleidoscopes
looking over vast turquoise turtle tortoise seas
mysterious silly yet slow serious silver transport
defying amber age wrinkled in rhymes
words shock like streaming purple pops
strained by delectable dots in skies of delight
sentiments far away scarred scarlet stars
blinking like slinky Christmas light bulbs twinkle
in tinsels tinkling wink to drip blue confetti tears
salted with experiences sweet apricot seeded
poetic peach tree expression for lovers only
raptured from pains of ordinary boring days
reinvigorated by this glowing glorious amethyst
joyful gemstone emerald ruby diamond delight
a flash flames to echo spring love discoveries
taken in and up on invisible wings for whimsy
to a place where ever color has a feeling
and every exiled purpose a proper partner
to share in risky rapture of escaping capture
within the grave grip of grey gravities below
no we go on friend never to worry ever again

The Need to Write
Matthew Burgio

I felt the need to write today
So sat down with my Scribe,
As the Sun was nearly setting
With the hope to catch a vibe.

The snow has nearly melted and
The breeze has no ill chill.
My skin soaks up the warming rays
Though winter tarries still.

I'll take respite, if for a day,
Enjoying thoughts of spring
And the rush of cabin fever
That the cold snap tends to bring.

I'm ready for more grilling and
More walks out at the park;
Some boating and some archery
And bonfires when it's dark.

There're even really basic things
When nicer weather's here
Like sitting out to read or write
Or just enjoy a beer!

For now I'll take what warmth I can
Both in the day and night,
And use this inspiration to
Appease my need to write!

On this Side of Heaven
Eric Aguilar

On this side of heaven,
my heart still pounds and beats.
The cars switch lanes and
poverty paves the streets.
On this side of heaven,
blessed are the meek.
One day they'll receive a mansion
catty-cornered to golden streets.

On this side of heaven,
the stars are in our view.
You walked on the waters
that separates me from you.
On this side of heaven, you are
the light that sees me through.
A beacon in the darkness;
In faith, I blindly call out to.

On this side of heaven,
scars are reminiscent of pain.
Flesh follows the fire but,
the spirit is washed by rain.
On this side of heaven,
many things lean and wane.
It's your word that changes me
yet, your word stays the same.

On this side of heaven,
the rich are those who give their last.
Who offers in joyful generosity
before the question can be asked?
On this side of heaven,
many stones are thrown and cast.
But, you show us how to forgive
with every mark, stripe, and lash.

On this side of heaven,
I surrender in trust.
For, you have purposed me
and purchased us by your blood.
On this side of heaven,
I thank you, Father, for your Son
who patiently picks us up
and graciously shows us love.

Gaps in the Sea Wall
Anna Treasure

I want to write a
poem as ferrous
and elemental
as the sea.

Although
the words
would be as
stark and briny
as a sea wall

the meaning
would be clipped
close to the wind,
barely existing.

It would ask
what happens
when man is
stripped before
the bottomless
merciless waves.

The gap in the
sea wall could

let in any
poetry and
flighty glimpses
of redemption.

But

I'm not tied
to a mast in the
Atlantic, I am in
Andalucia and

maybe the
dust motes
falling in
the evening
are more
truthful.

Maybe more
and less even
than that
is true,
maybe the
deafening
silence

in between
both the dust
and the breaks
in the sea wall
is all there is.

(And what is
redemption
anyway?)

Her Quiet Song
Leslie Clark Hicks

Still is the beauty of
quiet
        —its color calming
―

        mossy green is the path to
tranquility... fascinating

   and

   hypnotic
                bewitchery's song... it cries to
me,
   akin to the Siren's
song ...
        the forests green—
watching—
        it's magick all around me, humming an alluring
tune   —seductively
captivating,
        its Beauty sings of Serenity
―
   as the Knowing blooms inside of me
...
   Still—her quiet song.

Angels for You
W. Fields

as a baby's laughter melts the heart..
and their cries summons missions of love
just as waves from the ocean which models
the climate bears forecasts through supreme light above
bold eagles soar the current
that propels their strength anew
while succinct delegations..
in the midst..
have commissioned the Angels for you

as the road not travelled spawns legions of grief..
to annihilate your mortal soul
and the depths of hell plots a scheme
to siphon your Spirit and takes its toll
then your cries from the plague pierces Heavenly realms
that the Grace not be hindered from view
and enlightenment born from transcended events
manifest by the Angels for you

Angel Babies
Kirsty Howarth

I am your little angel
In heaven up above
Even though I was not born alive
You still showered me with love

I am still a part of you
And even though you grieve
In your heart I'm with you
And I will never leave

We have a special bond
And that will always stay
I am waiting patiently
For when we meet someday

The time you carried me
To me is very dear
And my love for you
Really is sincere

But in this life
I was never meant to be
And I know how hard it was
For you to set me free

When the time is right
Together we will be
You are and always will be
The perfect mum for me

The Rage
Taylor Juliet Ashton

boils from within
faster than I can say no

now
I can't handle
the heat that rises
from my chest
to my head

I am engulfed
in my emotions
a screech
from my innards
and I crumple under
my demon's weight

water appears
in the form of my tears

it's over before
it's even begun

Final Verse
Jou Wilder

I'm wound up in memories of us—
but this is the last verse I'll write about us.

I sever our ties—we go separate ways.
The arrows of deeds stuck to my soul
are plucked out by a blazing flame.

You and I fragmented in the heart of the sea.
I sprinkle the ashes of us into the wind
here by the shore where we both succumb.

I'm the first to bury us by this very sea—
the place where we both plunged
long before we drowned.

This is my final verse to you.
I bring to a focused completion
our shared memories.

The burning sensation is now at ease.
This is the summit of release—
my final verse of us.

About Wheelsong Books

Wheelsong Books is an independent poetry publishing company
based in the ocean city of Plymouth,
on the beautiful Southwest coast of England.
Established by poet Steve Wheeler in 2019,
the company aims to promote previously unheard voices
and encourage new talent in poetry. Wheelsong is also
the home of the Absolutely Poetry anthology series,
featuring previously unpublished and emerging poets
from around the globe.

Wheelsong has more poetry publications in the pipeline!
You can read more about Wheelsong Books and its growing stable
of exciting new and emerging poets on the
Wheelsong Books website at: wheelsong.co.uk

Wheelsong Publications

2020
Ellipsis by Steve Wheeler
Inspirations by Kenneth Wheeler
Sacred (2020, Revised 2024) by Steve Wheeler
Living by Faith by Kenneth Wheeler
Urban Voices by Steve Wheeler

2021
Small Lights Burning by Steve Wheeler
My Little Eye by Steve Wheeler
Ascent (2021, Revised 2023) by Steve Wheeler
Dance of the Metaphors by Rafik Romdhani
Into the Grey by Brandon Adam Haven
RITE by Steve Wheeler
Absolutely Poetry Anthology 1 by various

2022
Absolutely Poetry Anthology 2 by various
War Child by Steve Wheeler
Hoyden's Trove by Jane Newberry
Shocks and Stares by Steve Wheeler
Autumn Shedding by Christian Ryan Pike
Cobalt Skies by Charlene Phare
Wheelsong Poetry Anthology 1 by various
Rough Roads by Rafik Romdhani

2023
Symphoniya de Toska: Book One by Marten Hoyle
Vapour of the Mind by Rafik Romdhani
Nocturne by Steve Wheeler
Symphoniya de Toska: Book Two by Marten Hoyle
Wheelsong Poetry Anthology 2 by various
Constellation Road by Matthew Elmore
Beyond the Pyre by Imelda Zapata Garcia

Symphoniya de Toska: Book Three by Marten Hoyle
Wheelsong Poetry Anthology 3 by various
This Broken House by Brandon Adam Haven

2024
All the Best (Poetry 2020-2023) by Steve Wheeler
Invisible Poets Anthology 1 by Invisible Poets
Darkness into Light by David Catterton Grantz
Wheelsong Poetry Anthology 4 by various
Marmalade Hue by Donna Marie Smith
Melancholy Moon by Gregory Richard Barden
Average Angel by Matthew Elmore
Storming Oblivion Peter Rivers
Circus of Circles by Aoife Cunningham
Stealing Fire by Tyrone M. Warren
Wheelsong Poetry Anthology 5 by various
The Infinite Now by Steve Wheeler

2025
Creative Deviance by Steve Wheeler
Off the Top of My Head by Graeme Stokes
Invisible Poets Anthology 2 by Invisible Poets
Invisible Poets Anthology 3 by Invisible Poets
Elementals by Ryan Morgan
Wheelsong Poetry Anthology 6 by various
Bellowing to a Lost Echo by Brandon Adam Haven

Printed in Great Britain
by Amazon